PETER H. ROBINSON'S

THIRD BOOK OF GHOSTS AND HAUNTINGS

Researched & written by

Peter H. Robinson

HUTTON PRESS

1993

Published by the Hutton Press Ltd.
130 Canada Drive, Cherry Burton, Beverley
East Yorkshire HU17 7SB

Produced by

Burstwick Print & Publicity Services
13a Anlaby Road Hull England
HU1 2PJ

ISBN 1 872167 54 3

Contents...
...or your list of **ghosts and hauntings.**

INTRODUCTION

Well, here you are again, reading this my third collection of ghosts and hauntings and since that first collection was published in 1987 I don't think much more than a couple of months have passed when I haven't heard of a 'new' haunting, and even though many of these were used to make a second book in 1988 I still had stories to research for a proposed third book.

Once again I approached the Reverend Tom Willis who besides being Vicar of Bridlington Holy Trinity Church and of St.John's Sewerby, is also the official exorcist to the Diocese of York and as you will appreciate is a leading authority on the subject of the supernatural. I explained to Tom about the development of the third collection and asked again if he would like to add more of his experiences to my collection, and I'm very pleased to say he did.

Over many months we had numerous discussions on the subject of the supernatural and thankfully Tom always had a new haunting to tell, of these you will read on the following pages.

After three published works telling of the mysteries and fascination that surrounds a ghost story or haunting, I am still unable to explain the origin of a haunting, although a great many theories do exist, some having been described in my previous writings.

Early in 1993 I had the opportunity to meet a lady with firm beliefs in a life after death and shall in due course introduce you to her...

........We had finished the meal, and I was somewhat guilty of over-feeding my guests, (but to be honest no-one was forced to have 'seconds'). Coffee over, we sat with glasses of wine and relaxed and talked. Two out of my three guests I had not met before, and as such concerned myself for the after-dinner entertainment. I feared a boredom setting in fast, but I was well 'lubricated' with that gift from the god Bacchus and I 'subtly' allowed myself to relate a ghostly tale or two. My audience was riveted (well, politely they listened) as I unfolded chilling tales from my new collection. This in turn led to the inevitable discussion on the origins and reasons for ghosts and hauntings, each listener in turn contributing to the discussion. Then Paul said he thought I would be interested in meeting his mother, especially as she had a spiritual awareness and firm beliefs on the subject. Paul felt sure she would be willing to have a chat with me, and that she was, for only four days later on a visit to Hull from Lincoln I met Doris.

My evening in conversation with Doris was refreshing to say the least and brought back memories from my Sunday-school days and the teachings of good and evil. In Doris's own words I reproduce in part my interview with her...

"There is the good and there is the bad. The good is God. I see God not just as one figurehead, but the collective good of mankind that has gone before us. Evil is the Devil and that's bad." "We are two bodies, the energy body inside, that's the real us, it holding all our feelings, emotions, anger, pleasure and memories. Our other body is the flesh which of course deteriorates and dies. But because our energy form cannot be destroyed, it goes on after death merging in spirit with both conscious and subconscious, thus giving us a greater insight to anything we could ever have believed whilst on earth. And although spirit is everywhere, there is yet no single answer, and no distinct explanation for a haunting..." As already said, theories abound on the subject and many pages could be occupied raising questions and searching for answers, but whatever explanations I put forward they are little more than stumblings on a path to an answer. Reflect upon these and many past words and allow yourself to journey through my pages. And again I ask that question, dare you steal that glance behind?...... for who knows what or who lurks and moves in that dark corner, was it just a shadow or reflection on your specs ?.....

Peter Harvett Robinson, June 1993.

.....dismiss that shiver and
turn the page......

FOREWORD

How often do you visit the cinema, see a 'great film', and return home still thinking about it? A strange question with which to begin a foreword in a book that has nothing to do with cinema, I know. But bear with me while I ask another strange question along similar lines. How often have you visited the cinema to see the sequel to that 'great film' you couldn't stop thinking about, but come away wishing that it had never been made? I know I have.

"But what," I hear you screaming, that is if you're still with me, "has any of that got to do with this book?" Okay, I'll tell you.

In 1987, Peter's first collection of ghost stories was published, and judging by the way it sold I can only hazard a guess that you liked it. Then, in 1988, came the sequel - 'More Ghosts...', and you went back for more, impetuous little imps that you are. And now comes a second sequel, and look, here you are again! The only difference between that 'great film' sequel and this series of books is that although you have a rough idea about the plot you know that the actual storyline will be fresh, and therefore, hopefully, you will not wish that it had never been published.

To be honest, I know nothing about ghosts. In fact, I don't really know why I was asked to write these words apart from the unfortunate truth that eight years ago I was asked to write the foreword for Peter's first venture, "The Home of Beautiful Pictures", and at that time I wrote: "I'd never written a foreword, and probably now never will again..." and until this moment that statement had remained quite accurate. I can only presume (assume), as with the last time, Peter couldn't find "a suitably famous name", so here I am again.

I've read Peter's previous collections, of course, and I've even been on a tour of Beverley on the ghost walks they have inspired. I've seen television programmes which have tried to explain the phenomenon, and I confess to finding the subject fascinating. But I still know nothing about them. I've never seen one (as far as I know) and I've never felt strange chills, had a numbing sensation or turned white with shock at anything more terrifying than The Eurovision Song Contest, so what qualifies me to be writing this?

Well, I know that Peter talks enthusiastically and incessantly about the ghost stories that he has collected because I've heard him, and when I've returned to the land of the living (no pun intended) having drifted away from his ramblings following a glazing of the eyes and a dozing off sensation, he's still talking at me ... sorry ... to me about them, and eventually his enthusiasm for the subject can have an infectious reaction rather like a rash, it tends to get under your skin and there's no way of getting rid of it unless you agree to his bullying tactics and agree to do something positive - like write a foreword.

Anyway, with regards to this book, if you find that you have enjoyed reading this third collection of ghost stories then you'll probably demand a fourth (I shall be out of town that week), but until then you will just have to content yourself by re-reading it, or digging out (up) the other two to read again.

However, if by some chance you find that you're disappointed with this third collection then may I suggest that you go over to that table , with the broken leg, remove "The Home of Beautiful Pictures" which has been propping it up for the past eight years, replace that book with this one and then read that book again (always presuming that you did read it in the first instance).

Personally, and I was told to make this plug, you could always return this book to the shop from whence it came and politely ask if you could exchange it for a copy of "Last Complete Performance - In Memory of Hull's Cinemas". Why? Because I wrote that one.

ROBERT CURRY
August 1993

ACKNOWLEDGEMENTS

As before my list is lengthy, but without the help of those I thank I'm afraid this publication would not have been possible. Firstly, thanks to the Reverend Tom Willis who again has shared with me some of his haunting experiences.

To the following my thanks are extended for allowing me the privilege of access to a ghostly or haunting experience: Margaret Richardson, Andrew Train, Pat Gaden, Joan Lambert, Len Harrison, Gordon Jessop, Anita Wain, Elsie Williamson, Joyce Daddy, Keith Daddy, Dick Robinson, John Robinson, Brian Jackson, Paul Hesp, Robert Curry, David Bowman, Russell E. Hills, Val Peacock, staff present and past of The Hull New Theatre, and many more who wished to remain anonymous. My grateful thanks to you all.

Thank you Paul Schofield, my 'Ghost Host,' who walks Beverley's haunted and historical streets re-telling tales of the town's ghosts and hauntings, for Paul too has shared with me hauntings as told to him whilst conducting his walks.

For support and encouragement my thanks go to Doris Jenkinson, Paul Pritchard and Marcus Webster.

By now you must have realised that this publication in no way represents a 'one man show' - to the contrary, it's almost a 'cast of thousands'. Well, not quite, but my list of acknowledegments must continue and it's thanks to Steve Oldfield again not just for organising typing services but for some of his established and quality artwork. Thanks also to Robert Curry not just for his foreword, but a typing service and support, also Bill Jefferson for his typing services. And now it's that special thank you to our illustrators from the front cover of Julien Webster to my photograph by Paul Hamer on the back cover (well, I think it looks OK.!) and to those pages of quality illustrations between the covers, my thanks go to Adrian Durrant, Rachel Pamplin, Richard Desborough, John Regan, Tony March and David Barton.

And last but certainly not least my friends at Hutton Press, Charles and Dae Brook, who helped me bring the first two ghostly volumes to your book shelf, have again been instrumental in encouragement and support in making this the third collection of ghosts and hauntings available for your bookshelf collection.

Peter Harvatt Robinson.

THE STORY CONTINUES..........

Or the ghostly update, for that's what follows now, starting with Beverley's Cottage Hospital. In the first collection of Ghosts and Hauntings, we told of 'The Ghostly Surgeon' nicknamed George who was seen in a corridor gowned up and ready for theatre. Also a series of unexplained happenings affecting a patient call-system, mysterious door knockings and voices, all blamed on 'George'.

To continue with the Cottage hauntings, in 1988 Paul Schofield, who hosts our ghost walks around the town, had in one of his parties a lady who had worked at the hospital. She told Paul of the occasion she was in a ward on her own, when she heard a man coughing or clearing his throat, the sounds coming from directly behind her. She turned immediately to see who was there, but other than herself the room was completely empty. She continued her duties and made up one of the beds, but had to leave the room for a few minutes. Upon her return she was dismayed to find that the bedding of her recently made bed had been pulled back! Who was responsible? No-one else had been in the room, so again the blame was placed at 'George's' feet.

Still with 'George's' feet, it is believed that they were responsible for the footsteps heard on May 26th, 1990, when staff heard them very clearly 'walk' along the main corridor. The staff in the sterilising room fully expected someone to knock and enter. However there was no knock and no-one there, but those footsteps were heard to walk away! Sadly 1992 saw the end of the Cottage Hospital, now demolished, making way for a new housing development and, who knows, new homes to wander through for George!!

Moving into Beverley's Saturday Market and Edwards the Opticians at the northern end of the market place. A few years ago they had a 'visit' from a polite gentleman who actually apologised for having startled the lady cleaner one Sunday morning, then disappeared! But not all the happenings at the premises have been so polite or considerate, for it has been told by patients of the opticians that during the last war when the building was used as flats, a lady occupant awoke one November night to find 'hands across her throat' and a gentleman of no connection with the aforementioned lady told one of the partners in the business that he had experienced hands round his throat whilst staying there! Makes you shudder to even think about it.

To the southern end of the town and Well Lane where I was once led to believe this was the site of a plague burial pit, certainly not from the plagues that 'visited' the town during the years between 1604 and 1645, but possibly from a much earlier one. However, research furnished no evidence to prove that victims of a plague had ever been buried in the Well Lane area. Then an idea came to mind. It was not impossible for a Pest house to have occupied a site in Well Lane. These sad establishments were for the unfortunate plague victims who were isolated and invariably ended their days there.

It's only an idea, or at worst a historical guess, but could the existence of a Pest house in the area be an explanation towards the apparition that was believed to have been seen in a Well Lane house! For I was told of a man who appeared with a black bag who wore a mask in the shape of a beak. This description would fit a plague doctor or physician of the day who were often called 'Quacks' because of their beak-like face masks. Those beaks contained herbs and spices in the belief that they would protect the wearer. But what I didn't know, and thanks to someone on Paul's ghost walk, was that those medics or Quacks used sliced oranges in their beaks as well as the other stuff.

Now it's only another of my theories but if in those days past, they believed oranges offered some protective properties and if a Pest house had been in Well Lane, and oranges were used to protect, then could that be a possible explanation for the reports that a 'strong smell of oranges' has on occasions filled the air at number 13, the Age Concern Charity Shop?

Interesting theory isn't it? Regardless, I still do not like walking along Well Lane, especially at night. Does anyone else feel the same?

A few minutes walk away across Wednesday Market and into Highgate towards the Minster. Highgate was at one time called Londoners Street, and according to George Oliver's much respected 'History and Antiquities of Beverley' published in 1829, Highgate was, during the plague, blocked off at both ends by barriers and to quote Mr Oliver "The dead bodies were now conveyed in great numbers through the yard of the George and Dragon Inn (The Monk's Walk), and buried in tumuli in a field adjoining the outer trinities", under what was the old coal depot and present Railway Station. In the second ghost collection we told of the Monk's Walk hauntings, which may in some way have connections with those sad, dark death-filled days of the plague. But besides our 1986 record of hauntings, mysterious footsteps were heard in 1989 by a member of staff, and again in May, 1990, when Roy heard footsteps in the passageway which runs the length of the building. On this occasion Roy thought the footsteps heralded the arrival of a member of staff, and called out to her, saying she was early. There was no answer and the door didn't open to reveal who Roy expected. Somewhat puzzled he went out to investigate, only to find no-one there! A check of the toilets also proved negative.

For those readers familiar with the Monk's Walk and to dispel any thoughts of those phantom footfalls belonging to someone taking a short cut between Eastgate and Highgate, there are doors at each end of the passageway that are locked outside of business hours and on both occasions were locked!

Still with Public Houses, this time past the Minster but practically in its shadow is number 13 Flemingate, or the Lord Nelson and believed to date back to 1620. In Ghosts II we reported a presence that caused the occupants and their dog to feel uneasy along with unidentified footsteps.

In 1989 the Nelson changed hands again. Within three months of the new residents arrival, strange things began to happen.....

The December 14th, 1989 edition of the *Beverley Target* carried on its page 2 the headline "Ghostly Goings-On in a Beverley Pub", with a sub-heading "Lord Nelson - A Pub that's got Spirit"! This proved compulsive reading, though sadly no apparitions had been seen. How disappointing I thought, but this time things had gone beyond the sound of footsteps and that feeling of a 'presence'. The published list of strange and unaccountable happenings now reads quite extensively.

The landlady had been imprisoned in the kitchen, even though the door wasn't locked she couldn't get out. One night a pack of pork scratchings exploded, scattering its contents over disbelieving customers. Light switches would not respond to the landlady, but did for her husband! Various articles disappeared and re-appeared in already searched places. The one-armed bandit, no lightweight to move at the best of times, has moved on its own accord overnight. Probably even stranger was the mysterious appearance overnight of an old, discoloured pewter teapot not seen before by staff or the cleaner, who had been there years. But that teapot one night appeared to 'jump' from the shelf hitting a customer on the head as it fell.

To date no explanation is available for these oddities, and there is no known history of violence or unpleasant deaths there, but then you never know what's under the floor or in the walls do you!? And if those walls could only talk!.....

Now that I have brought you up to date with the additions to our previously recorded hauntings, I would like to invite you to share with us any new haunting experience in properties that already are reputed to be haunted, then hopefully on re-prints of this publication we can continue to update this section.

On to what I believe is a record of some of the better and most interesting ghost stories, hauntings and other strange happenings that I have managed to access and the many that my good friend the Reverend Tom Willis has been involved with.

We hope you enjoy sharing with respect our 'haunted' pages.....

THE REWARD

As many readers will already know I have been involved on a part-time basis with Beverley's Playhouse Cinema since leaving school and have managed the business since films were re-introduced in April, 1982. My full-time employment was at Westwood Hospital, where I worked as Hospital Cashier and Bereavement Officer up until February, 1990.

However it's at the Playhouse where this story begins. Paul Hesp, the Cinema's Assistant Manager, and myself had in 1987 successfully brought together our first collection of local ghost stories and hauntings. It was only weeks after the first book went into the shops that the problems started. You may not think being given money is a problem, but when you don't know where it comes from, well, that's different......

At the time we were screening the film *Snow White and the Seven Dwarfs*. It was Sunday, December 20th, and we were not particularly busy. Following the usual system to balance first the ice-cream monies, then ticket sales, take out float, finally drinks, and whatever is left represents the night's sweet sales. Our years of experience had given us the ability to estimate, to within a few pence, the sweet sale figures. So imagine my surprise when on that Sunday my sweet sales were a few pence over £27! It couldn't be right, £7 yes, I knew I hadn't sold much more than that. I mentally totalled the sales and arrived at a figure very close to £7, that meant I was £20 over! I checked all my figures and money again, all were exact as before!

The next question I asked myself was who had I short-changed? Could it have been four at £5 or two at £10? Impossible. I called Paul through and explained my problem. His attitude was to a degree sympathetic, but tinted with a bit of ridicule at my 'error(s)'. The surplus cash was put to one side in the hope that at the week end balance its appearance would be accounted for. But it wasn't.

The following Thursday I was at the hospital preparing the cash for banking. The receipts totalled £449 but to my horror the actual cash totalled £499. I was exactly £50 over! Where had I gone wrong this time? Or who had I robbed? I remembered the previous Sunday and that £20. Was my mind going?

Every receipt was double checked, I thought I may have entered a wrong amount. In panic I called the District Cashier who came down and went through everything with me, but still its origin was untraceable. His suggestion was to keep it in the safe in case a possible solution arose. If not, pay it into the system at the end of the financial year.

The mystery remained, who had slipped me that £50? The cash box was kept in a locked safe and strong room and I had the only key! So in less than a week I had mysteriously made £70!

I had almost forgotten my 'ill gotten' gains, until my colleague Paul reminded me about my problem with the cash. Surprise! Surprise! It had happened to him on December 28th after balancing. He too found he was £20 over and a thorough double check still didn't make any difference. He too put the money to one side in case an error showed up later.

One day at the end of February, I returned home after a trip to Scarborough. My meal was in the microwave, a tray sat on the draining board. 'That's odd' I thought, who's left a £10 note? There it was under the rim of the round tray at the 12 O'clock position. A brand new £10 note gently rolled up in such a way that the Queen's head was fully displayed facing upwards.

An inquest followed, it certainly didn't belong to me or anyone else in the house, so who then had put or left it there? That note was a conversation piece for days, but still no-one wanted to own that orphan note - so I adopted it.

Now if you have been keeping a tally you will have realised that the 'free' money had totalled exactly £100 and still without an explanation of origin.

The Playhouse money, after a respectable waiting period, went into a paint and general improvement fund and the £50 'found' at the hospital was paid into the system at the end of March.

So just where had the money come from? Was it a thank you from our ghostly friends?

I discussed the matter with Reverend Tom Willis, who thought it was not impossible for it to be a 'thank you' and even suggested it could be the late proprietor of the Playhouse, Mr Symmons, expressing his thanks for our efforts in maintaining the cinema. If that was the case, where had he got the money from? Tom's next suggestion left me very uneasy – had his widow had a similar amount of money disappear? After all, what she had could have been his also– I dare not ask, and to this day I haven't.......

COINCIDENCE OR PREMONITION?

Although this book is principally a collection of ghost stories and hauntings, I felt the inclusion of my experiences with premonitions would not be amiss in such a publication.

At some time or another, many of you will have experienced that feeling that something is, or was going to happen and it did. Unnerving isn't it? Probably a better understanding may be deduced from what I tell you here.

I looked up the word Premonition in my Collins Dictionary, I found the following that besides being a noun it means 'Previous warning or information, an instinctive foreboding'.

I had for a long time felt that my mother had a sort of sixth sense and to a certain extent felt that somehow I had inherited a similar sort of ability as has my brother.

Mum often had feelings about people and so often those friendships I valued could be undermined with comments on their reliability as friends and could tell which and how they would let me down. I never took this too seriously, but as I look back now, I do not recall an occasion when she wasn't right.

Confirmation of that sixth sense became evident in August, 1981 when it appears mother felt a 'warning'.

I was at work when mum phoned to ask me if I could get some time off during the afternoon to go into Hull to see a friend who was very poorly in hospital. I asked why. She just said she thought I ought to go before it was too late. Had she had a phone call from my friend's wife, I asked. Her answer was 'no', she just thought I should go if I could. I did, my friend was indeed poorly and back home and about an hour and a half later, I received a phone call to say my friend had died!

Mother had her favourite spot, it was a place in the countryside on the River Hull at Brigham Lock, and when standing on the bridge looking up river she said she could just visualise Ratty and Mole crossing in their boat, the scene was so idyllic.

I had decided to take mum to her favourite spot on the Thursday night. She stood and stared gently absorbing that page from 'Wind in the Willows'.

On the Saturday following, I journeyed up to Pickering to video the North Yorkshire Moors Railway. My intention had been to complete the return trip on the next but one train after looking round the loco sheds, but before I had even arrived at Grosmont, I felt I must return on the next train. I would complete my round trip, return home and cut the lawns, thus leaving Sunday afternoon free to take mum and auntie out for a drive. I don't know why but I felt I had to.

The afternoon was fine and sunny, mum and auntie walked under the blossoming cherry trees in Langton, then round by Kirkham Abbey to Malton then home.

Just over 24 hours later mum was rushed into hospital where she remained to her death a week later. Amidst the sadness I felt I had given mother a last few hours pleasure through our country drive. Had I been somehow warned?

As the months passed and the weeks ahead would bring round the first anniversary of mother's death, I suggested to auntie that we did a 'pilgrimage' to Langton to coincide with that Sunday visit one year previous. I didn't know why at the time, but for some reason I changed my mind and went a few weeks earlier. No sun this time, just heavy rain.

A few weeks later I felt I should buy myself a new bathrobe and when I decided I had to have one I felt I had to get it with a degree of urgency.

What a coincidence, and it didn't dawn on me until weeks after. On that Sunday when we should have done the 'pilgrimage' to Langton, I was admitted to hospital with a heart attack and needed that new bathrobe! Coincidence?

Then one night during my convalescence my brother and I sat watching TV when out of the blue he asked if I had seen or heard anything from Adrian. I asked which one. As he said which one of the two he meant, there was a knock at the front door followed by a tap on the window. It was the Adrian we hadn't seen or heard from for well over a month!

Well, what do you think? Coincidences, premonitions, sixth sense or whatever, as individual occurrences they probably don't amount to much, but when studied together I feel they are more than coincidences.

Stop and think of the times something similar has happened to you. Did you regard it as coincidence or what?

RELATIVES

Relatives, what are they? Just in case you have forgotton, they are the members of your family, mums, dads, aunts, uncles, gran, grandad, niece, nephew and so on. To some they can be interfering old busybodies, to others they love and care, to many of the young they can be a pain, but remember you too are a relative of someone, so how do you think you fare in their eyes? Are you a pain in the bum to someone in your family? and how much love and care do you give and take? Think about it!

Whatever answers or conclusions you arrive at we all have or have had relatives and even in death it appears they still care or want to know what's going on in the life they left.

Tom uses the term 'good dead' to describe the visiting or caring relative and I feel it's an appropriate title. For example there was the man who went into his office one day and to his surprise behind the door stood the ghost of his late father! Or the lady who told of her husband coming downstairs looking as though he'd seen a ghost, enquiring what was wrong, he told her he had been getting something from a drawer, turned round and came face to face with his deceased father, who spoke saying, "I've just come to see how you all are, oh! sorry, I'm frightening you" and disappeared!

Or the relative who comes to 'say' goodbye as happened to the man who lived in Hull's Sculcoates Lane and worked at the nearby power station. He was noted for being a 'bit of a lad', liked a drink and readily admitted to not believing in a great many aspects of life, but underneath that hard and jovial exterior, there was a good and serious side to him. Life obviously wasn't easy because of his wife's illness he had had to bring up his four son family.

One night this man awoke from his slumbers to see there in the bedroom his youngest son. But that was impossible, that son was out fighting a war in North Africa. A few days later notification arrived from the War Office advising that his youngest son had been killed in action and the time of the son's death coincided exactly with that last farewell visit of the lad to his father!

PART ONE: HAUNTED BEVERLEY

THE KING'S HEAD - THINGS TO COME?

How often have you wished you could see into the future? Probably even a small peep would sufice, but then would you really want to know what lay ahead? For me, I'll settle with the past and leave the future until it arrives!

But for one family who came to Beverley for the first time, they were given what is believed to be a rare treat. Still puzzled by their experience at the King's Head when back at home, the lady sought out the Reverend Tom Willis and phoned him telling of their family's brief peek into the future.

The family comprised of husband and wife, along with her mother and father. After leaving their home in Essex, they had arrived in Beverley during the late afternoon, in time for afternoon tea before being shown to their rooms.

During tea, the waiter told them "you will be having your meal through in that room there" and pointed through the room they were in, through into another room. The lady, her mother and father all saw a very attractive new and modern room, the decor being of wood and red leather and tables beautifully set with tablecloths and sparkling glasses all ready to welcome the would-be eaters. They commented upon how nice the room looked (although the husband has no recollection of looking or seeing the room at all).

Refreshments over, they retired to their rooms, unpacked, then went out for a short walk round Beverley. Upon their return they readied themselves for the evening meal, but on their arrival at the intended eating place were surprised when they were shown into an entirely different room to the one they had seen before. This room was older, quite reasonably furnished but in much older style. Nice, but begining to look a bit shabby.

Towards the end of their meal they asked the waiter why they were in a different room to the one they had been shown earlier where they were supposed to have eaten. The waiter, puzzled, listened intently to their description of the mystery room, but the King's Head didn't have a room that remotely resembled the one they described!

Conversations then developed between other staff, all equally puzzled but curious to find a solution to the mystery of the missing room. They then went back into the room where they had earlier had tea, showing staff where they sat and explained that they had looked through from there into the room as previously indicated. Silence descended on the family as this time they didn't see the wood, red leather and tablecloths. This time it wasn't there, all they saw now was the room in which they had just eaten!

Sometime later in a conversation with the manager, he said it was strange that what they had seen and described to him was how the room hopefully would be after refurbishment! So what explanations for this phenomena are available? How or why did three people have a peep into the future and apparently see the same picture? Coincidentally though, a week before their visit the Hotel had hosted a Clairvoyants conference! Or had they actually experienced a time-slip and seen the room as it is in the future? Or had they somehow accessed the minds of the designer and, or the manager, both of whom knew what the place would look like eventually?

It's a mystery, strange but true. But as a footnote to this story it has also been reported that in recent years someone saw an upstairs room from the past looking distinctly Georgian or Jacobean!

THE VICTORIA BARRACKS GHOST

Years ago before Victoria Road, Beverley, became the busy brightly lit main road it is today, a lorry driver was driving along the dimly-lit street when a man appeared to run out from the disused Army Barracks (now demolished), straight out into the road in front of him. The driver braked and looked around for the man who had seemed to stop in the middle of the road, waving his arms. The man was nowhere to be found.   On asking around, the lorry driver heard rumours that a man (soldier?) from the Barracks had been killed there years before.

ANOTHER SOLDIER?

Still along the Victoria Road and the sighting of another soldier.

Elsie was baby sitting in one of the flats belonging to the old Army Barracks on Victoria Road, when suddenly there appeared a soldier dressed in a First World War uniform.

Elsie was surprised, but not frightened. She spoke to the apparition and as she did it gradually faded and disapppeared.

Upon his return Elsie told the man of the house what she had seen, but he wasn't in the least bit perturbed, going on to say the ghostly soldier was quite a regular visitor and believed it to be the ghost of his father who had been killed during the first war.

Needless to say, as is so often the case with a ghostly sighting, no-one believes you, Elsie's husband being no exception, but Elsie assures me that the soldier wasn't a trick of her imagination.

ANOTHER NORWOOD HAUNTING

I had heard murmerings about the haunting at number 34 Norwood, so was not surprised when the story of this haunted property appeared in the 1988 edition of the *Beverley Journal*.

No. 34 is an Army Surplus and Bikers supplies store run by Andrew and Yvonne Wood with partner Tim Coles. No-one to date has actually seen a ghost in the premises, but there is certainly something strange resident there that makes its presence frequently known, although whoever or whatever remains a mystery.

Heavy and substantial boxes that could not possibly fall from a shelf have been found removed and placed in the middle of the floor. Had they fallen they would have ended up almost below the shelf, but not these boxes. Motor cycle spares have also been moved around, yet never damaged. However, this ghost also makes itself known by switching off the showroom light, gently closing the door and manages to activate the electronic sensors that are only sensitive to heat and movement!

On one occasion the staff were with a customer downstairs, when suddenly a series of loud thumps were heard moving across the floor upstairs. On investigation it was discovered that an Army helmet that had been secured to the wall "had been bounced across the floor".

Although the ghost has not been seen by the staff it is thought that Jennifer the two-and-a-half year old daughter of Yvonne and Andrew may have seen something, for one day they found her looking towards the ceiling pointing and laughing. "She was fascinated" Yvonne said,"there was definitely something there to hold her attention, but we saw nothing". When Jennifer's parents asked her what she could see, Jennifer pointed to the ceiling at the same time saying "look at the pretty lights" yet nothing was seen by anyone else.

No-one is unduly frightened by the happenings at number 34, but all are reluctant to venture upstairs to the showroom at night and as for the dog – it keeps well away!

ST MARY'S MANOR

I seem to recall it was during the early eighties when I had first heard that the manor had a ghost, but sadly had never been able to track down any details until one Sunday morning four of us were on a pre-season ghost walk round Beverley. One of our party, Robert Curry, asked if I knew of the haunting from the manor. I didn't and so in Robert's own words you too can discover the ghost of St Mary's Manor.

"In 1983, 1 was working for the Ministry of Agriculture, Fisheries and Food, which was based at St Mary's Manor, North Bar Within, Beverley.

I was fascinated by all the little back stairways that linked the corridors of one section of departments with another, and in particular with one that had a door in the wall.

When I asked about this, I was informed that it was a store-room, though years earlier, when the house had been a private residence, it had been the bedroom of some servants. The room itself wasn't very large, and I was horrified to discover that it had no windows.

I was further told that some members of the cleaning staff were reluctant to perform their duty on this particular staircase because of a certain uneasiness they felt in the area. One lady had already reported her unease by relating her story.

One evening she had been going about her work quite normally. When she began to clean this particular staircase, she suddenly felt something brush her shoulder. She turned, expecting to see a colleague, but saw no-one, so dismissing it, she continued, but the brushing against her shoulder occurred again. This time she felt a shiver and quickly finished her work and then left the area.

It later turned out that she hadn't been the only one to have had this experience, and others who hadn't even been brushed against often complained of a coolness in the area. Investigations revealed that a young servant girl had once hanged herself on the staircase, and it is believed that her ghostly presence creates the coolness. It is also believed that her swinging legs are what has been felt brushing shoulders."

A HOUSE IN MILL LANE

Betty Spence had kept her story secret fearing it could upset the present occupants, then as a result of one of my appeals for more hauntings, Betty wrote to me. As on previous occasions and for the respect of the present residents, I am not revealing the house number, but will identify it as a house in Beverley's Mill Lane.

The year was 1972, Betty and her boyfriend had spent eighteen months gutting and refurbishing the house, her boyfriend doing most of the renovation work himself, but was always 'apprehensive' when alone in the house. Especially when on the first landing at the top of the stairs the strange discomfort he felt worried him so much, that he was embarrassed to admit it existed. But there was something odd about the bedrooms. They were always cold, even when the rooms were heated!!

About six months of married bliss passed quietly, then things started to happen. One Saturday lunch-time, Betty arrived home from work to discover the doors locked, repeated knocking didn't bring any response from her husband, then peering through the front room window she saw him sitting apparently sound asleep. Knocking and banging on the window didn't arouse him. As Betty says "it was as though the interior of the house was completely sound proofed." In desperation Betty called her father-in-law who had to break a window to gain entry. Even the noise of that didn't wake the sleeper, only a good shake did, all he knew was that he had fallen asleep!

Unnerving things now began to happen. At 2 a.m. the door bell rang several times, investigations revealed no-one there or anyone in sight. It happened again, in fact it continued for a week always at the same time, 2 a.m. The prospect of it being a practical joker was dismissed, was it faulty? Possibly, so the batteries were taken out, but that wasn't the solution! the bell continued to sound at 2 a.m. every morning! - that bell was removed and disposed of.

But that wasn't to be the end of their problems for the final straw came when Betty was woken from her slumbers by an ice cold hand on her face. At first she thought it was her husband, but he was asleep with his hands under the covers, the time was 2 a.m.!! Betty was confident their home had "more than an earthly presence" and persuaded her husband that the time had come for them to leave that house, which they did.

Now I found this story fascinating, because of similarities I discovered from another house in Mill Lane, the story being told in my second ghost collection (page 30). I am sure the houses are one and the same, as it's rather coincidental that the lady occupier in that story experienced a hand touch her face, and one of her sons had seen something on the landing. Unfortunately I have no record of that house number, but the similarity of that touching hand is uncanny isn't it?

THE GREEN DRAGON

I always think The Green Dragon is an attractive looking pub and although somewhat 'squashed-in' by the surrounding higher buildings still manages to project its charm into Beverley's Saturday Market. Though giving an external appearance of being small the visitor will, when inside, find it surprisingly large. Now I could ramble on for many more lines extolling the virtues of good beer, food, biergarten and decor, but then you may begin to wonder why I am not writing for a pub guide instead.

On now to the history of this pub; records go back to 1746 when the building on this site was known as the Malt House and only re-named The Green Dragon in 1765, so as you will appreciate a building of this age should have a ghost or be haunted, and yes, to qualify for entry in this publication it does have a ghost and is haunted.

Now before I tell of this, I suggest we have a brief peep into this pub's past in an attempt to identify any events that could give rise to the happenings that occur therein!

During the last two wars it was a very popular pub frequented by the locally barracked military personnel, but then most town pubs with a military presence nearby benefited during wartime.

Back now further (oh! for that time machine) to 1689, and legend tells of an ale house once on the site of the present building where a view would have been had of the last public beheading, this taking place on the Cornhill; the 'unfortunate victim' being a Danish Mercenary who was executed for the killing of his Comrade (worthy here is mention of a plaque commemorating the fight, situated on the south wall of St Mary's church), but even that event does not give background to the Green Dragon hauntings, although the building's recent alterations could possibly be a source of disturbance.

By now you must be curious to know just what has been going on there. Well, as hauntings go it's not one of the most dramatic I have reported, but sufficiently disturbing to cause the staff a fair degree of anxiety.

Steve Oldfield 1991

Jane phoned me one pleasant July afternoon with distress in her voice. Something definitely was not well with her, she went on to explain that one of the staff had just seen a ghost!

For quite some time Jane had suspected that their pub was haunted and that they had ghost, this being attributable to a number of inexplicable switching on of lights and interference with the cooker controls, but an actual sighting was the needed confirmation that they had a ghost.

The staff member had just gone through the door into the passageway, when suddenly the figure of a man "shot" past her and into the new bar. An instant realisation dawned on her that the figure that passed wasn't real, and from Jane's description she definitely looked as though she had just seen a ghost.

Investigations were to reveal that no-one had entered the new bar or at least no-one of human form.

Jane then went on to tell me of the potato incident when a bag of potatoes left on the sink side burst into flames without any apparent cause or reason, necessitating a 999 call to the fire department who could find no explanation for the occurrence. Then there was the nephew in the kitchen who saw clearly a dial control on a cooker turn round on its own!

To date no explanation has been found to account for any of these happenings, or who the ghostly man could be, but I left Jane reassured in the knowledge that should they be 'visited' again or the disturbances continue then I would recommend contact with the Reverend Tom Willis who I felt sure would bring peace back to The Green Dragon. One year on I have heard no more, but now with alterations completed those disturbed spirits may all have settled to their new surroundings.

THE PUSH INN

Only a stone's throw away from the Green Dragon we find another haunting. The Push Inn is Located next to the PIayhouse Cinema on a corner site overlooking the market place and incorporating an off-licence. In 1991 changes to the property were planned which may have been the cause of disturbances within the building.

In their book, 'The Inn places of Beverley', Frank Pinfold and George Higginson comment on the pub's unusual name, "it is claimed", they say, " that there is no other pub in the country with the same name" and that the name originates from having swing doors with the word "Push" painted on them. During the Playhouse's 'Bingo' years the Push was very convenient for bingo players who were thirsting for a drink between games. They could simply come out of the side exit, cross the narrow passage between the two buildings and enter the pub via a side door. Perhaps it didn't help them to play any better but it made them happier about, losing.

Over the years there had been rumours that, the Push was possibly haunted but it wasn't until the new landlord came forward with an account, of his experience, in the summer of 1991, that, I had anything of substance worthy of inclusion in a ghost story collection such as this one. His telephone call was to reveal a series of inexplicable occurrences within the premises.

One of the earliest, incidents of note was the night, when the landlord and four friends were sitting in the downstairs bar eating a pizza after the pub had closed. As they tucked into their late night feast the last thing on anyone's mind was a supernatural intrusion. It was a very down to earth group who sat and ate, and it included an army sergeant, but conversation stopped dead when an unfamiliar

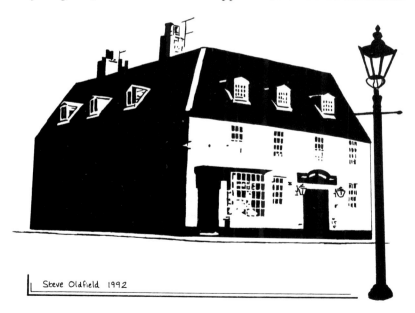

Steve Oldfield 1992

27

voice was heard to say "I know! " Who knew, and what did they know'? Certainly none of the humans present had an explanation for this eerie disembodied voice.

Lights and bottle tops featured in the following incidents which took place in the pub cellar. To quote the landlord, "Everybody feels strange when they go in the cellar – all the staff have said ' I don't like going in the cellar', and one of the lads, Ian, an ex–RAF man, he'd been down there one night and he came up and said 'OK who's playing silly fools turning the lights out', but, everybody was rushed off their feet so we said 'Nobody's been down the cellar, we all knew you were down there changing the lager or whatever!"

Ian then told how as he approached the lager the lights went out and plunged him into darkness! He made his way through an adjoining door to the bottle store and turned the lights on again but as he reached the lager someone or something turned them off again. All the staff were working up in the bar effectively ruling them out from interference.

Bottle tops with a life of their own were encountered by the landlord and his staff on numerous occasions but the landlord's wife was sceptical until one Monday night when she and her husband were in the cellar.

Bottle tops are generally kept in a skip in the bar area until being disposed of. Any stray ones are picked up immediately to avoid people slipping on them. So it came as rather a surprise to hear a bottle top clunk on the cellar door then roll under the door (which has a 3 inch gap for drainage purposes) and down into the cellar. "There you are," said the landlord to his wife, having experienced this sort of thing before, "Explain that then!" She naturally assumed that there was someone at the top of the steps playing tricks but on checking found there to be no – one in the bar area.

On an earlier occasion the landlord was sorting through some crates alone in the cellar when a bottle top came clinking down the stairs. Thinking it was probably the children playing tricks he put his head round the door and shouted up to them telling them to stop and warning them of the risk of people slipping on discarded bottle tops. The landlord turned back to the work he was doing and two more bottle tops came bouncing down the stairs, so again he yelled up the stairs issuing a final warning to the children. No sooner had he resumed his work than it happened again.

"The third time," he says, "it was like a big handful.... so I went charging up the stairs and I said 'Right, that's it!' I walked in behind the bar and of course there was nobody there ."

He checked both toilets and all around the bar believing the children might be hiding there. Then he rushed upstairs to the living quarters, passing through the kitchen where his wife was preparing breakfast, and found his two children laying on the foor watching television. They denied all knowledge of the incident whereupon his wife confirmed that they had been with her all the time!

Curious though these incidents are, perhaps the most disturbing aspect of this haunting concerns visitations to the children's room by a mysterious grey-haired and bearded old gentleman who forewarns the children that their parents are about to come up and check on them.

According to the landlord the old man, who has so far appeared three times, does not seem to frighten the children in any way but is accepted as a kind of grandfather figure.

The old gentleman appears in the children's bedroom which is situated in a developed part of the attic, the rest of the attic area being unused. "He comes through the landing door, the cupboard on the landing. It would make sense to me by thinking that it adjoins the old quarters that haven't been altered."

The ghostly visitor has appeared to the children on three occasions to date and holds conversations with them as the current landlord relates. "He said to Gareth 'Your doggy doesn't, like me', so Gareth had said 'She will do when she gets to know you, she doesn't, like misters'. The old man replied 'Oh no, she doesn't like me. Pussy cats don't like me."

On one occasion the dog was accidentally locked in a room in the pub and when the door was eventually opened she bolted out, terrified. Perhaps she saw the old gentleman too.

So who is the mysterious gentleman? Investigations into the history of the pub have provided no clues.

The landlord is of the opinion that the cause of these events may be connected witih the discovery of some old duty and excise documents which had apparently been hidden in the pub many years previously. Was some long-hidden secret in danger of being revealed?

Or perhaps the proposed alterations to the property may have disturbed resting spirits. We may never know the real truth, but one thing is certain the ghosts are not malevolent, rather they are playful and, in the children's case, protective spirits. Should the property be exorcised? As in a number of other hauntings, this family are happy to leave well alone.

A GHOST IN TIGER LANE

It was whilst on one of the three ghostly walks of York that I had my first serious thoughts about Beverley's Ghosts. I was sure that with diligent research I could unearth a few good hauntings to qualify Beverley for a Ghost Walk or Haunted Trail.

I was lucky, having my own to tell from the Playhouse and with a few initial leads to follow I quickly built a trust with people prepared to tell and share a ghost or haunting. With the quality of story, and a great many from people's personal experiences, I realised that the quantity of material received could be more than a foundation for a walk but would write up well into book form.

Months passed and more stories than would fill one volume made preparation for a second a possibility – I had a wealth of hauntings to share. With the first book published in October 1987, I spent the winter months planning the most interesting route round Beverley to include some good hauntings and historical sites (although the two do link well together).

With script, book and town map I set off with a colleague to pace out my haunted trail. A cold Sunday morning in February is not the best of times to stand around telling ghost stories, but at least we planned a route and ran up a good time. Slight modification to the script, include more historical fact, and I felt we could present something to the paying public comparable to York.

Next I needed a 'ghost host' or someone to walk a paying public around the town.

Sadly I didn't have the time (although I did take the inaugural party) so I advertised for a 'ghost host'. "Strange job to advertise," they told me at the job centre, "Will you be employing them?" they asked me. "Well sort of," I replied, "you see they will be using my researched material and effectively employing themselves."

The applicants were interesting, but I settled on a chap with just the right qualifications and interested in tourism which was of course the market I was entering. We met and took the walk one wet July night in 1988 and within weeks Paul Schofield had become Beverley's official and first 'Ghost Host'. It is now three years on and besides the walk, 1991 has seen the introduction of the Historic Haunted Trail, taking in the north and west sides of the town.

Now as Paul tells our tales, from time to time he collects other people's, and although my previous words outlining the history of the walks may be many at least you the reader have a background to the origins of both books and walks.

After all that I had better allow you access to one of those stories Paul was told, and in his own words.....

"As Beverley's official 'Ghost Host' I often feel somewhat privileged when people on the ghost walks tell of their ghostly experiences and in some cases they are very personal to their witness.

One story I was told during 1989 I will now relate to you. The witness to the apparition was a lady instructor of a Yoga class in certain rooms in Tiger Lane.

The ghost first appeared as she was trying to create a relaxed atmosphere and at the same time issuing various instructions to the class. Without doubt the sudden appearance of a figure in front of her brought surprise to say the least! It was dressed in a habit with hood reminiscent of that of a monk or friar. Very shaken she tried to continue the yoga session as normal, desperately trying not to disturb the assembled group, but at the same time still strongly aware of the ghostly stranger's presence. Eventually the figure disappeared, and the session continued.

However, the instructor had not been the only person to see the stranger, for upon leaving, one member of the group hesitantly explained that during the session she had watched in total disbelief the appearance of the Monk or Friar directly in front of the instructor. This brought a degree of comfort to her for it then confirmed that the figure hadn't been a figment of her imagination alone, but the question remains unanswered, who was the ghostly visitor to the Yoga class?........"

PART TWO

HAUNTED HULL
THE GHOST OF ST PAUL'S

Even though I have heard of numerous haunted churches, to me, it somehow doesn't seem right for a church to have a ghost, but it happens, as in the case of our next story.

Hull's St Paul's Church in Sculcoates, had been around for a good few years and had served the community well in life, so why shouldn't it be a refuge or home for someone in death?

St Paul's Church was demolished in 1976 but before the building became a memory Tom Willis was to discover its ghost.

It was soon after Tom had become vicar of St Paul's that he was to learn that the church was haunted. Tom dismissed the legend, at the same time adding that many old buildings had reputations for being haunted. But that wasn't the end of the matter, for Tom was told by a number of people that they had seen a figure standing beside him at the altar when he had celebrated Communion, but always, it disappeared as he approached the Prayer of Consecration, while Tom saw nothing at all and doubted that others had too!

A family friend making her first visit to Hull came to stay with Tom and his wife. Her journey had been a long one, and decided an early night was needed, but before retiring enquired as to what time she should be up for breakfast. Tom told her there was no rush for he had Communion at seven o'clock and would, if she wished, wake her upon his return. "No!" the visitor said, she would like to attend Communion also.

However, during the service Tom noticed a strange reaction from his guest, for when Tom reached the part where he said "hear what comfortable words our Saviour Christ says......" That he noticed her suddenly look up and look to her left and stare goggle eyed. She was obviously watching something, her eyes following a movement. Tom continued with the service, at the same time looking to see if he could see what the woman was watching, but Tom saw nothing at all and after the service neither he, nor his guest, made any mention of the happening.

The Friday morning brought with it a repeat performance of the previous Wednesday. Tom was taking the seven o'clock Communion, the guest saying she would also attend. Again it happened, but this time further on in the service and as Tom said "Hear also what St Paul sayeth....." She suddenly looked up and followed again nothing with her eyes. Tom continued with the service looking in vain to see if he could see what she saw.

Back home after breakfast, Tom said to his guest "You saw the church ghost did you?"

With a sigh of relief she replied "Ah' Yes, and you saw it too did you?"

Tom answered with a firm "No. I just watch people watching it!" He then went on to say that for some time he had noticed members of the congregation looking or watching something other than him. He then asked her to explain what she had seen. Her description told of a small woman dressed in Victorian clothes who seemed to appear from beside Tom as he stood at the altar, then walk down the aisle.

So who was this ghostly lady? Or who had she been in life? And why was she still around? Some said she had been a previous vicar's wife and her grave was at the rear of the old abandoned chancel that had since been cut off and awaited demolition of the church.

Tom went to investigate, to find no grave, just a metal plaque to commemorate her and put there by her husband who had been the first vicar of the parish, his wife having died about five years after he had taken up the post.

Later, in discussion with another previous vicar of St Paul's, Tom was to learn that there was a grave there belonging to Hannah Kemp-Baily, wife of that first vicar.

That set Tom thinking, and hearing others say they too had seen things, he decided to ask some of St Paul's other clergy about this legend. Tom spoke to four who had all been at the church before him, even one who had been there during the nineteen thirties. One dismissed it as rubbish. Another said that he too had heard the same, but he too dismissed it. The third said he had a feeling there was somthing there and it could explain a lot.

Now the fourth, who was somewhat of a 'toughie' having previously been an ex-major in the Army, had also been told the church was haunted – and dismissed it also as a load of rubbish – that was until the day he met an old lady' He had gone through into the old vestry. Now this room only had one door and provided the only way in and out. Upon opening that door he was amazed at what he saw, for there standing with her back to him, was a little woman looking through the drawers. So with hands on hips he bellowed, in his best military voice, "What do you think you're doing?" With that she disappeared' She didn't pass him and remember there was no other way out! A few months later he saw her again 'flitting' in and out the pews.

The question was asked again, could the church ghost be that vicar's wife, Hannah Kemp-Baily? Some had thought it was, saying her grave was in the chancel.

Sometime later, one Saturday night, Tom suddenly remembered that he hadn't marked the place for the Sunday reading. It was about 11.30 pm and realizing it was late, thought he had still better go and do it otherwise he may forget in the morning. He went into church, put the lights on, straightened out the altar and marked the Sunday reading, then reflected on how lovely and peaceful the building was at that time of night. With that he began to have a strange feeling. He nicknames it the 'zig zags' around the edge of his body, probably defined better as a slight electrical feeling. Tom left the altar and went into the vestry walking quite boldly through the old vestry where the lady had been rooting through the drawers and into the abandoned part of the church which was spooky, shadowy and a chaotic mess of rubbish, on into the chancel where he had found the commemorative plaque of Hannah and where her grave was believed to be. Tom stood there, his 'zig zags' coming to a crescendo. He was mystified as to what was happening and felt as though something was about to happen, at the same time aware that the only light in that room came dimly through a glass partition from the church. Fear crossed Tom's mind at the prospect of someone coming into the church and thinking the lights had been left on and switching them off. Then without a second thought Tom spoke to the grave, apologising for the place being in such a mess adding that he would get it cleared up, at the same time offering a blessing to the grave.

Returning to the altar, Tom continued straightening it off. Suddenly he stopped to ask himself why he had just done what he had? And with that thought in mind he left hastily for home.

When Tom reflected on that night, he felt he was somehow drawn through to the grave and ended up blessing it also apologising for the mess there was, which was later cleared up.

The story continues now with a lady who, having plenty of time to spare, was taken on to help around the church; she cleaned, polished and generally helped out to keep the church looking good. At one time the lady had been involved with the occult and admitted this to Tom who had strongly advised her against dabbling, in or with it. She agreed. She wouldn't. However, Tom was to discover from his 'cleaning' lady that she too had seen the ghostly little woman and also a priest with a smile on his face had appeared to her one day as she cleaned the Kemp-Baily chalice! She wondered if the ghostly priest could have been that previous departed vicar of that same name? Tom discouraged her thoughts and feelings in that direction.

One day the lady came to Tom and begged him not to show any anger if she admitted something to him, Tom agreed. The lady went on to explain how the people next door had had a medium in and she was invited round.

During the proceedings, the medium addressed the lady saying that she had a woman 'there' who kept saying 'Harriet, Harriet' and is polishing something. Later, the cleaning lady was to ask Tom if Harriet was the woman who was buried in the old chancel.

"That's where you're wrong" laughed Tom "because her name's Hannah, it's in the back of the baptism book." Baptisms had been crossed out and burials added. He showed her, number one, Hannah Kemp-Baily, wife of etc.... and signed by her husband, thus confirming that she was buried there and substantiating that the name was Hannah not Harriet.

Anyway Tom and his cleaning lady decided to have another look at the plaque. They discovered it was loose and so took it out and proceeded to clean it. The letters had worn badly but they could still read the name Hannah, made up as 'H' and 'a' a stroke and a curve made the two 'n's', a blob which was thought to be the 'a', another upright with a bit attached which must be the 'h'. It certainly looked like Hannah. But as the cleaning and scrubbing continued the name became clearer – 'Harriet' They looked at each other in amazement.

So what had gone wrong? The plaque said Harriet. The floor was the original Victorian one. How on earth could her husband have walked over it with the name being wrong, the name on the plaque must be right. So why was the name in the book in the vicar's handwriting Hannah? Something was not right. Was this the reason behind the cleaning lady being told the name 'Harriet' and 'to polish', for doing just that had revealed the name Harriet. Could this account for the ghostly lady's wanderings and search in the vestry?

A check with the newspapers of the day still came up with the name Hannah Kemp-Baily. The question niggled away. Why the different names?

Further investigations followed through the Hull Library with the discovery that during the 1870's a survey of Hull churches was done. The researcher recorded that 'over the grave of the wife of the first encumbant is a large carved stone with the words Hannah Kemp-Baily along with her date of death.' Realization of what had happened then dawned, for around the turn of the century a new inlaid floor had been put down on top of the original stone floor and it's here that the mistake was presumably made, for either the engraver of the metal plate had been given the wrong name or he mis-read the handwriting, or was it because over the years the congregation had worn away some of the letters, giving the impression of the name being Hannah. Whatever the explanation the wrong name had been put on the grave!

When the old church was demolished and the new church built, the grave was then outside, so Tom insisted that Hannah's grave be marked with a new plaque with her correct name on and a hope that the little ghostly Victorian lady would rest in peace with her correct name marking her last resting place.

Still at St Paul's for our next haunting, but this time it's a phoney. I was surprised when Tom asked me if I would like one for the collection, so here it is. Try to visualise the scene and appreciate how unnerving it was at the time and what a tale could have been told it Tom hadn't put the lights on.

Very late one night Tom went into the church and was surprised to see that the aumbry in the wall where the sacrament was kept was without its flame. However, a flame was there, wandering about some seven or eight feet above the altar; up and down it moved. Tom's first reaction was that in his rush into church the darkness had caused his eyes to go a bit wobbly. No, the flame is not where it should be and it is drifting around on its own. Tom was convinced he was seeing or about to see his first ghost. Then his scepticism took over, the thought now 'if it is burning, am I just seeing an image or is it really there, and if it's there, what's it burning? A wick? The wick must be in a candle, so what's holding the candle?' He visualised a disembodied hand' With that thought, Tom worked his way along the wall in the dark to the light switches, flicking the whole lot on in one go, flooding the church with light, and what do you think Tom saw? There, hovering on the altar steps was a drunken man holding a petrol lighter' and by coincidence the aumbry light had gone out. If Tom had fled in fear at the first sighting of the wandering flame and not discovered its origin, you can easily see how, once the story had been told, without its druken explanation, it would have added to the church's already haunted past.

THE HEADLESS GHOST and others

The year was 1968 Joan worked at the British Cocoa Mills in Tower Street. One day while sitting in the dining room, Joan's friend came in looking and sounding upset. "I'm leaving here" she said and went on to explain that whilst she had been packlng on the conveyer belt, someone had thumped her on her back, but there had been no-one there. Now Joan's friend worked alone, so it was definitely not attributable to a fellow workmate. The incident distressed her so much that she said she was leaving. Joan begged her not to go reminding her that she wouldn't get any wages – regardless, she left, Joan taking her place on the belt.

What happened next stuck in Joan's memory to the extent of her memorising the season, day and the time. It was one Wednesday during the summer at about 3 in the afternoon. Joan was packing nuts for the Rowntree sweet factory at York, suddenly she felt the temperature around her begin to fall to almost 'freezing', but for some unknown reason she glanced to her right and there in a moment of time stood a 'headless' man, 'slightly built' and of a 'humble posture'. To make matters worse, Joan felt sure 'he' knew her. The shock was too much for her. She left the belt and fled up to the factory where work stopped as the distressed Joan walked through. This unfortunate event necessitated her being sent home sick for two days.

Upon her return to work the manager was reluctant to believe Joan's story. Her foreman remained strangely silent on the matter, but her 'forewoman' took Joan to one side and admitted that she too had seen the headless apparition!

Yet another confirmation came to Joan's ears, from her daughter-in-law, She had heard of 'him' being seen six years earlier in 1962.

Joan bravely continued working at the factory for quite some time and she too felt a 'thump on her back', but on that occasion thankfully saw no-one.

Joan told me that the headless apparition was reported to have been seen about five times and although it is not known if his appearances contiued, someone felt it necessary to make a small cross which was placed near the packing conveyor belt, presumably in the hopes that it would lay the poor man to rest. Unfortunately I do not know if his appearances ceased as a result of this move or not.

One thing is certain, poor Joan never forgot the day she saw a headless ghost.

As soon as that story was typed, I sent a copy to Joan for her to confirm that what I had written was accurate and at the same time I asked if she could indicate the possible origins of the apparition. Sadly Joan passed away on December 2nd 1988, but before her death, Joan had started to reply to me. Her letter and very brief details of other hauntings were found, whilst the family sorted through some of Joan's papers. The letter is reproduced in part as follows:

"Thankyou for your letter. It is accurate and very pleasing. No I know nothing else about the apparition, but there had been a dreadful fire at the cocoa mllls, and I think lives were lost."

I was fascinated by Joan's other notes of hauntings and dearly wished I could have accessed them earlier and in more detail. However, scant as the information was, Joan had heard of a ghostly surgeon at the Hull Royal Infirmary on Anlaby Road, who assisted by putting instruments in their correct order.

And during the last war, there had apparently been a gunsite in the vicinity of Meaux Abbey. Joan had been a gunner there with the 511 Battery and had been told of a mischievous ghost who roamed the site. (Could it possibly have been one of those monks wandering around? We have already reported one seen during the 1930's.)

Still with the war, but back in Hull, and a voice heard in a cellar, counting one, two, three and so on, Joan wondered if this may have been the ghostly voice of someone counting the bombs as they fell.

Then followed the strange experience from one of Joan's friends. The day after the funeral of her husband the house became exceptionally cold and a sweet smell permeated the rooms and the presence of her late husband was felt; then followed the appearance of the lady's son Lee, who said "all was well", but Lee had been drowned in a drain near Lorraine Street about 28 years earlier!

Joan's notes included other hauntings, but were unfortunately of insufficient detail to use. However, I am grateful to the family for forwarding them on to me.

THE BRITISH COCOA MILLS

Returning to Tower Street and the Cocoa Mills, this time with a haunting that is believed to have very tragic origins invoiving the death of a whole famlly.

Joyce Daddy worked at the Cocoa Mill in the early '70's for about four years as a "nut picker" when the incident that follows happened.

It was one morning whilst Joyce was walking down a passage connecting the yard and the toilet that she saw a grey-haired old woman appear from an outside wall. Around her shoulders was a shawl, but as she walked towards Joyce it became apparent that the old woman was dripping with water.

Joyce stood transfixed as the woman came within a few feet of her. Then turned and slowly retraced her steps back along the passage, disappearing through the wall again, the other side of which was the bay where the barges unloaded the nuts for the mill.

As you will appreciate, poor Joyce was terrified and wasted no time running back to her workmates where she attempted to explain what she had just witnessed. They tried to calm her wlth a cup of tea and an aspirin while other workers admitted they too had seen that same woman. This comforted Joyce to a certain extent, knowing she wasn't the only person to have seen the strange woman.

However, one employee who had been at the mill for a great many years offered a possible explanation. It appeared that many years earlier two children, a girl of 4 and a boy of 6, had fallen overboard from a barge into the River Hull. Sadly their parents arrived just in time to see their children disappear beneath the murky waters and an adjoining barge drift across filling the gap where the children had fallen.

In a desperate attempt to save the children, both the Mother and Father dived into the water..... they were never seen again.

It was assumed they were either trapped beneath the barges or were stuck in the notorious silt on the river bed.

The bodies of the two children were recovered by rescuers on the river bank and were taken to a room in the Cocoa Mill.

The girl was already dead and her brother died shortly after. The man who told of this tragedy also claims to have seen two young children in the mill and believes both they and their mother may be wandering in search of each other. But so far no-one claims to have seen the children's father in the building, or have they? Remember our other story from the Cocoa Mill, a few pages back, and the headless apparition of a man – well, are you now thinking what I'm thinking?

THE HOUSE IN EXMOUTH STREET

I couldn't for one moment think who could possibly be writing to me from Australia, New Zealand yes, but Oz, no.

The envelope was addressed to 'The Authors, Hauntings of Beverley and East Riding'! Could this be my first Australian ghost story? As I massacred the envelope, I visualised the next ghost book, 'Ghosts and Hauntings of Beverley and other parts of the World', well, it was only a thought.

The letter was from a Brian Jackson ex-of Hull and now living in Australia and told of many strange happenings in a little old house in Hull's Exmouth Street. I found it a fascinating tale, but am certain of one thing; the house appeared to be a pleasant normal peaceful place, that is until the occupants tampered with the supernatural, and I believe started the chain of incidents you are about to read. Believe it or not, there are many dangers associated with this sort of practice, as you will discover, so beware and leave well alone. Brian's story now follows and I felt it should be told in his own words. Read now the mysteries of 'The House in Exmouth Street'.

"I was recently in England on holiday, in the course of which myself and a couple of friends went on the Beverley Ghost Walk. During the walk I chatted with the guide and told him of some of my experiences with a ghost (or ghosts?). He was most interested and suggested that you too may be interested.

When my wife and I married, we lived in a house in Exmouth Street, off Newland Avenue, Hull. We moved into the house in June 1960 and for the first few years nothing untoward occurred. However at New Year (not sure if it was '64 or '65) we held a seance, using a circle of letters and figures, a wineglass and a polished table; the usual

40

nonsense was spelt out, though one bit of sense did emerge. The glass spelt out that a friend of mine who was present at the time, would within the year meet a girl whose name would be Sue. They would have to get married and have a child. At that time nothing was further from his mind, but within the year, what the glass had spelt out came to pass. Anyway, to go on with the story of our hauntings, a couple of months after the seance, odd things started to happen.

Firstly, an ornamental plate that had been hanging on the hall wall, fell soon after my wife and I had gone to bed for the night; nothing strange about a plate falling off a wall you might say, but the strange thing was that half the plate was up against the front door and the other half was nearly at the top of the stairs! We thought it a bit peculiar, but put the accident down to traffic vibration, though that did not explain how the pieces had landed where they had. Around the mid-sixties manufacturers used to give away plastic flowers with packets of washing powder and my wife had collected a few of these. On the top landing (the house had two staircases) we had a small cupboard on which my wife had placed a vase with those plastic flowers in it. One night whilst going upstairs, I found the vase balanced on the bannister rail. Our first thoughts were that someone was fooling about, and as we had a couple of children, they became prime suspectcs. However, that vase was moved on numerous occasions until we got so fed up with it, that we put it away; but that wasn't the end, A flower from a vase of real flowers from the kitchen was found on my wife's pillow; an umbrella, which had been missing for some time, was found on our bed when we awoke one morning.

Now follows the saga of the light bulbs. On the top landing was a ceiling light fitting, very high up (children could not have reached it). Well one night I went to turn the light on only to find that the bulb had disappeared! We racked our brains trying to account for the disappearance of that bulb and could come to no other conclusion other than supernatural interference. At this point I should add that neither my wife nor myself had any belief in ghosts etc, more the opposite! To return to the light bulbs, a new one was fitted and the following night it too was gone. A further bulb was installed, and it also vanished a couple of nights later. None of those bulbs were ever found. The next thing that started happening was the wet beds. We would go to bed, only to find the sheets and mattress saturated, there were no signs of the bed having been disturbed and usually (though not always), the top covers were dry. If you think about this, it meant that whatever was perpetrating these acts, had the ability to insert the water in between the eiderdown and blankets without spilling a drop. The alternative was that the top covers were pulled back, the water poured on the bed and the bed remade! A rather tidy spirit don't you think!

As a result of my wife talking to a local shopkeeper, who just happened to have a friend who was a reporter, the story got into the *Hull Daily Mail* and the *Hull Times*, and that in turn got the spiritualists interested and involved, resulting in several seances being held in the house. On one occasion the medium had gone into a trance, she then started talking in a hoarse voice and said her name was Ada, and was apparently my wife's great Grandmother. When asked how she died, she said "the man made the horse go too fast and I fell off". Now my wife had never known her great Grandmother, and didn't even know her name, in fact she had never given her a thought. Of course we made enquiries with my wife's family and apparently her name was Ada, and she did indeed fall off a horse; however, it was a horse at a fair in Beverley, not a real horse, but one on a roundabout. I should also add that we had the local vicar in from Saint John's church at Newland, to conduct some form of cleansing service in the house. However, he did not believe the happenings to be of a supernatural origin and suggested to a neighbour that it was "that poor woman's husband that was responsible" in other words, me! Now whilst it would have been possible for me to do some of these things when my wife's back was turned many times things happened when I was not around and sometimes when no-one was in the house at all. I can assure you that neither my wife nor myself were responsible for any of these occurrences. Anyway despite the vicar and the spiritualists' best attempts, things continued to happen.

One evening my wife was taking a bath (the bathroom was downstairs) and she asked me to go to our bedroom for something. When I reached the door and tried to open it, I found a resistance from the other side of the door. On pushing the door more heavily, I was able to get into the room. The inside was a mess and the reason I had difficulty entering the room was that the mattress from our bed was upright against the door! The bed itself was vertical and the wardrobe was leaning against the window with its doors open and its contents laid all over the floor. Now the interesting thing about this occurrence is that my small daughter was asleep in her cot in the room, and had not been disturbed. I shot down the stairs to tell my wife. She in turn called her aunt who came down to the house and was shown the state of the room. Auntie was a Catholic and said there were no such things as ghosts, but was unable to offer an explanation for the happenings, whilst she helped us tidy up the room (by the way my daughter woke up the minute we started to clean up); Auntie was the last person out of the room and before leaving, she scattered Holy Water on the bed. An hour or so later we thought we heard a slight noise and went upstairs to the room again and found the bed once more disarranged. The top covers had been dragged back slightly as though 'it' was about to have another go, but had been disturbed when we went up the stairs. On another occasion, a friend of ours, Beryl, had come to the house to have her hair set (my wife was something of a hairdresser). The three of us were in the lounge, Heather, my wife, said it was a bit cold and would I get the heater from the front room, but when I opened the lounge door, which Beryl had come through only minutes before, the little cupboard from the top landing was in the hall outside the lounge door! Now I opened the front door to Beryl and we had both walked down the hall and into the lounge together, and that cupboard had certainly not been there then. So in that short space of time we were together in the lounge, this cupboard had 'travelled' down two flights of stairs and into the hall! And we were the only ones in the house. That little cupboard full of blankets, was rather heavy, as I discovered when I was putting it back.

On another occasion. Fred and Sue, who were lodging with us for a time, had gone to bed, It was Winter and they were cold. They came down again for a hot water bottle and a hot drink. No–one left the lounge during this period, but when they went back upstairs the bedding had been stripped and tied in a knot! Fred used some very strong language. The next week the spiritualists held another seance, and when the medium went off into her trance. she turned to Fred, and said "did you mean what you said the other night when you swore at me". The medium had not been told of the bedding incident! We left the house in 1969 and things were still happening. though of a minor nature. The house was sold to students from Hull University, and as far as I know there have been no occurrences since we left. Neither my wife or myself were at that time particularly interested in ghosts or the supernatural. However when faced with facts of the happenings in Exmouth Street, there seems little alternative but to accept a supernatural explanation for them. How else can they be explained?"

A fascinating story from Brian and in support of his uncanny experiences, he gave me names, addresses and telephone numbers of those people who besides himself were witness to those happenings should I need confirmation.

Brian's story was politely tidied up, typed, and sent off to him for his approval. A week later he replied as follows: "Thankyou for the copy of "The House in Exmouth Street", I am perfectly happy with the alterations you have made and eagerly await its publication. Whilst talking to my former wife recently, she brought to mind another event that happened about a year before we left Exmouth Street......

"One Saturday afternoon both my wife and myself had gone shopping on Newland Avenue, leaving no–one in the house. On our return we found that the mantlepiece in the lounge was wet. On looking up we saw water dripping from behind the cornice of the ceiling on all four walls and on further inspection found the carpet and furniture were also wet. My first thoughts were that a pipe had burst, as the pipes from the back boiler were in the ceiling space between the back bedroom floor and the lounge ceiling."

"However, on checking the back bedroom, we found that the water had apparently emanated from a box bed in the room. This was a single bed, the bottom section of which was a box in which to store clothes, blankets etc., on opening that box, we found (and judging by the water mark) that it had apparently been half full of water, and the clothing in there was saturated. Incidentally, it was not at all evident that the water had come from the bed, as the bed was made up, and the wet patch on the floor was not visible until the bedcovers were lifted. I had in fact lifted a floorboard and found no sign of a leaking pipe before we even looked at the bed. I would estimate that it would have needed about six buckets of water to have produced the same result! As there were no taps on the upper floors of the house, it would seem that whoever or whatever perpetrated the deed, had carried the water upstairs from the kitchen or the bathroom, or had produced the water out of thin air!"

Ater reading Brian's letter, I pondered for a few minutes. An Idea came to me, could this house have been so old that its owners once had maids? Had that back bedroom once been the bathroom? and was it possible that some poor servant girl or maid in spirit continued to fill what may have once been a bath?

I replied to Brian acknowledging with thanks his letter and addition to his experiences.

How had all that water got there? Like Brian, I too was puzzled, I wondered, was it possible that sometime in the distant past that bedroom had been the bathroom, and was the water carrier some poor long departed maid whose spirit still went about her duties filling the bathtub? It was only an idea, and so in reply I suggested this possibllity, and at the same time asklng if he knew any history of the house. Late January 1990 brought Brian's reply as follows:

"Thankyou for your recent letter, I am glad you found the water in the bed story of interest. What has always exercised my mind in relation to that story, is not so much the event in itself, but rather the mechanics involved to produce the large amount of water.

What I mean is, where did the water come from? Did this entity go down to the bathroom or kitchen and having produced a bucket out of thin air, then proceed to fill it at least six times and make six trips up the stairs and fill the bed? It would have also had to strip and remake the bed as it was still made when we entered the room. The alternative is that the entity snapped its fingers, (figuratively speaking) and Hey Presto! the bed was full of water! The mind boggles! Incidentally going back to the previous account of the wet beds, I should also have told you that on one occasion, we were able to collect a small amount of the water off the bed. This was given to the spiritualists, who told us that they had had it analyzed and that it was water with a slight concentration of Uric acid!

As regards your suggestion of a ghostly maid still going about her duties, I rather suspect not, for when those houses were built about 1908, I imagine they would have been occupied by the upper working class, whom I doubt would have employed a maid. I am also certain that when the houses were built, that they did not have bathroom. When we first moved in, the bathroom had been installed in what was obviously the rear bedroom and looked to have been a fairly recent addition. In fact I moved the bathroom downstairs into what had originally been the wash house However, whilst they may not have had a maid, they may have had a tin bath which had to be laboriously filled with water. It does stretch the imagination to think that they would add to the labour and carry the bath and water upstairs. By the way, the only room that was not affected by water or wet beds, was the back bedroom that had been the bathroom when we moved in. In fact as I recall, the only thing that ever happened in there, was the tying of Fred and Sue's bedclothes in a knot.

Another point which I have only just remembered, is that whenever a room had been disturbed, the atmosphere seemed to be intensely cold. This may have been entirely our imaginations at work, as when you discover something inexplicable like a bedroom disarranged, when you know it was alright a few minutes earlier and no-one could have been in the room. One does tend to get Goose Pimples! ! !

Anyway Peter, I hope the above has been of some interest to you and if there are any other details that I can help you with, please let me know."

Sadly, I could think of nothing further to ask Brian, and so came to an end of our ghostly correspondence, but I am left wondering about that house, if it is still there and what tales would the occupants have had to tell since Brian left

THE GHOSTLY RESIDENTS OF NUMBER 97

I first heard of these hauntings through a colleague at work. Pat is a forefront figure in the St John Ambulance Brigade and told me that their Hull headquarters in Spring Bank was haunted and suggested I contacted various St John's members should I wish to discover more' Of course I did. But my research was thrown out through me having to spend a spell in hospital. However, that didn't prove too detrimental for it was there that I met one of Pat's St John's associates, Andrew Train. We chatted about the haunting at the headquarters, then a few weeks after my discharge Andrew phoned to tell me more and put me in touch with those who had the first hand experiences.

No misty or vague shapes here, as I was to soon discover, but 'real' ghosts that may be as old as the building itself.

Gordon Jessop, also part of the St John's team told me first of his experiences. It was sometime during the mid-eighties, Gordon's wife was painting a door, whilst he was working in the hallway. He turned to speak to his wife and in doing so saw a maid suddenly appear. She walked from out of the back door and disappeared through the wall into what would have been the original back yard. This hadn't been a fleeting glimpse of the ghost for Gordon, for then followed his description of her clothing. Her dress was black and ankle length, a small hat adourned her head, whilst a smart white apron added that final touch. But even though Gordon's wife was there she saw nothing but added that she thought her husband was hallucinating.

But it appears that the maid isn't the only ghost to walk those halls, for then I next spoke to Len Harrison, who told me what he had seen prior to his retirement from St John's.

Len had often wondered what the headquarters building had been like in days past. After all it was over a hundred years old. It could have been a day when such thoughts allowed him to 'peep' back in time, for on this particular day when Len opened up the building and entered he saw before him at the top of the stairs a beautiful stained glass window, which he hadn't seen there before and didn't see again!

Apparently the window had once been made of stained glass but was believed to have been replaced with clear uncoloured glass either before or just after the last war. But on that one occasion the house let him see the window as it had once been years earlier, his description fitting that of someone who had once seen the original at the top of the stairs.

However, the window wasn't all Len saw for a few weeks Later whilst walking through what is now the shop he had the strangest feeling there was someone else in the room with him, although he knew there wasn't. Still he felt sure he was being watched accompanied by a slight chill in the room. Then, suddenly a woman appeared. Silently she walked from what had been the kitchen to the basement stairs, oblivious to Len's presence, although he did admit to feeling as though he were an intruder in *her* house and time.

I was curious, could this have been the same ghostly maid that Gordon saw? Not according to Len's description of her clothes, although she wore black ankle length dress and bonnet, but was without an apron. Len had the impression this lady had, in life, possibly held a supervisory position in the household, either as housekeeper or cook!

I found this haunting fascinating. How I envied Gordon and Len seeing those ghostly ladies apparently going about their business, and Len's bit of time travel, but he tells me he knew of someone else who also had seen the coloured window.

I couldn't help but wonder if those ladies still walk the halls and if so who do they wait on now?

THE WARNING?

After my chat with Len Harrison who told me of his experiences at 97 Spring Bank, he went on to tell of another haunting, this time from

Cottingham and South Wood Hall Farm, a place where as a child he had often played.

Apparently the farm was part of the old Priory which the farm had once supplied with milk.

Len went on to tell of the little girl aged about eight who whilst playing round the back of the farm had seen a strange man standing near an old water pump. The girl ran to tell her mother, who checked and found no-one there. The man was seen again by the girl who told her mother that he wore a red cloak like a monk's habit.

Mother's advice was not to play round there again at least not on her own.

About a month after a second sighting the girl's father was returning home and noticed that there were some severe cracks in a paving stone on the path near the pump. He poked and prodded around, until suddenly it caved in revealing a deep well underneath! After the well had been safely secured the strange man in red was never seen again by the girl.

One school of thought was that the 'man's' appearance served as a warning against the potential danger that lurked below that cracked paving stone, the consequence of which could have proved fatal had the girl fallen through.

MORE MONKS

Following on from that warning tale come more reports of monks being sighted around the same area. Now before I continue I would just like to confirm that historical records have established that a Haltemprice Priory was founded in circa 1324 and remains exist as part of Haltemprice Farm, off the Abbey Lane at Willerby. Whilst evidence also proves that there had been an Augustinian Priory attached to Cottingham and was founded around 1324, worthy of note is the fact that Augustinian Canons were of a very strict order, became very wealthy and built great monasteries.

The story I am about to relate comes from eye-witness Alan Batson, and I shall allow his experience to be told in his own words.

"It had been my usual practice to take a daily walk along the bridle path between Wold Road and Priory Road. On this particular morning I was scanning the fields for any sign of wildlife, seeing nothing of interest I turned in the direction of a nearby wood where, much to my astonishment, there stood in the entrance to the wood, and certainly no more than 150 yards away from me, a monk ... in a black habit, and it was almost as though through having seen me he had to leave, for he turned and walked away into the wood."

Here in Alan's story he admits that having had his Weetabix for breakfast he set off to run to catch up with the monk. Alan continues.

"...I checked the fields at each side of the woodland entrance then went into the wood, but he had completely disappeared, and there was no doubt about it, had he been there I would definitely have caught up with him well before he reached Priory Road!"

Continuing, Alan went on to tell, not this time of a personal experience, but of a nervous and upset lady who had met not one, but three monks!

"I was going to visit my wife who was a patient at the Castle Hill Hospital, and so walked on the path towards an old farm which can be seen on the route to Cottingham. As I walked along I noticed a lady walking towards me. She looked strangely agitated and nervous and kept looking over her shoulder as if checking to see if someone was following her.

Somewhat concerned for her welfare I enquired as to if all was well with her. Even with her odd behaviour all was right except, that is, that she was very nervous of meeting three monks she had met along that same path two year's earlier. Apparently, three monks had passed her walking towards the farmhouse and each carried what appeared to be a bowl and leaving a very nervous and frightened witness to take that short-cut home."

I've made this comment before, but I feel it worthy of repetition and that is how strange I find it that these monks or Friars, but certainly men of God and church, should still be wandering this earth. I thought by virtue of their vocation in life that they would have found peace and rest in death.

A NASTY ACCIDENT - TWICE!

A SHORT STORY NOW FROM EAST HULL.

As the result of a couple of strange accidents in Wincolmlee, a Hull taxi firm requested its drivers to avoid driving in that area after midnight. Apparently the reason behind this request was that one night a driver was going down Wincolmlee when a man suddenly ran out in front of his cab. Screeching to a halt the driver felt sickened at what he would find under or behind his vehicle. He got out to investigate but found nothing. He carried out a thorough search which proved negative, there wasn't even a mark on the bonnet. Back at the office, even though he was ghastly pale and very shaken up, no-one believed his story. That is until it happened again to another driver two or three weeks later. The same story repeated itself; a man ran out, the cab hit him, this driver too expected to find a body - and again there wasn't one. The strange thing is neither driver realised at the time that they hadn't heard a bump as the cab hit the man!

A possible explanation for these incidents was that it was thought both drivers somehow picked up the memory of an accident that had occurred in that place sometime previous.

YE OLDE BLACK BOY

For those unfamiliar with this quaint old public house let me introduce its situation within the city of Hull, and I must admit until late 1992 I hadn't a clue where the Black Boy was, let alone its established and prominent position in The High Street in the city's Old Town.

My sources tell me that Ye Olde Black Boy is the oldest public house along High Street with origins dating back to recorded use in the 1730s as a coffee house, but its use has been chequered since those days. Some say that the premises had strong links with the slave trade, but this is disputed as Hull was not known as a slave port, but then legends and hauntings so often run parallel in historical research.

From coffee house to pipe shop, snuff and tobacco sales and a corn merchants and during the last century the upper room was used for cock fighting. Our history told, I will now relate to you the hauntings as passed on to me by city tour guides Keith Daddy and Paul Schofield.

The first incident occurred late one evening. The landlord's wife, Sheila, was clearing away the dirty glasses from the back bar, but as she approached one of the tables to remove some glasses they suddenly began to shake themselves upon the table and to quote Sheila's words it was as if they were "dancing upon the table."

Later that same evening, the landlord, Bill, was working behind the bar and reached up to take some clean glasses down from upper shelves. As his arm stretched forth a bottle of whisky which stood next to the glasses started to move and shake about by itself, but so violent was this shaking it caused the bottle to burst spilling contents and glass over the shelves and glasses!!

Some time later, and a new landlord: He had just ended his first evening in charge of the Black Boy, last customers out and with a sigh of relief, he locked the front door, switched off the lights in the front bar and was about to do the same in the back bar, when he thought a re-arrangement of furniture would benefit the bar, and so he changed around the tables and chairs to suit, turned off the light and went to bed.

However, the following morning his efforts had been in vain, for all the tables and chairs had been placed back into their original positions, but under one table was the landlord's dog cowering and shivering with apparent fright. It was obvious something had frightened the poor animal. Whatever it was the dog went on a downward path never recovering and as such had to be destroyed.

Now to conclude this record of known hauntings is a tale to chill, for as I tell it I remember that I too have sat in that same bar, and although I liked the pub I somehow didn't feel comfortable. Back to that evening: A lad sat alone one summer night in the front bar, the night was warm and bright, so the landlord hadn't felt it necessary to switch the lights on, but even with the good evening light coming in through the window, with the dark wall panelling that surrounds the room an overall gloom was present in the air. The lad sat in the corner near to the bar flap sipping away his pint of lager. The longer he sat the more aware he became of something behind him, but he was next to the wall – nothing could be behind him. These thoughts were dispelled as quick as they came to his mind, for as he turned an uneasy glance behind he saw hands appearing from the back wall panelling. They emerged almost to the elbows and then retracted. The lager drinker didn't finish his pint. He left the bar at speed and was last seen running down High Street and to the best of the researcher's knowledge that lad has never returned to Ye Olde Black Boy.

Well, I am sure I shall visit The Black Boy again, but one thing is certain, I shall choose my seat with care!

52

HAUNTINGS AT THE HULL NEW THEATRE

According to the researched works of Robert Curry, and recorded in his book, "Last Complete Performance – In Memory of Hull's Cinemas", people have been gathering on the Hull New Theatre site from as far back as 1831, when at that time the building comprised of a 'large room known as the music room', whilst on the second floor was a lecture room, but sadly the interior was destroyed by fire in 1891.

Subsequent rebuilding brought with it balconies. Four years later, in 1895 moving pictures were introduced and in 1910 a cinematograph licence was granted. By 1919, the building had become known as the Assembly Rooms New Picture House. In 1924, a repertory company was formed becoming a private limited company, and live theatre was at last established.

As the threat of war arrived in 1939 the Assembly Rooms were converted into The New Theatre. 1951 brought the property into the purchase of the 'Whitehall Theatre Company'. Then in 1958, the threat of bingo loomed, but was kept at bay, and three years later in 1961 the Hull City Council purchased the building and still own the Property at the time of writing.

With that brief history of the Property known as The Hull New Theatre it will be realised that over those many years millions of People must have passed through its doors and into that hall of entertainment, so is it really surprising to discover that the theatre is haunted?

I shall say no more, but now pass you over to Val Peacock, one of the New Theatre's house managers, for Val has kindly researched and recorded the theatre's hauntings and now tells of them in her own words.

"CHARLIE"

"For heaven's sake, come in!" I shouted, glaring at the closed door opposite my desk.

There was no way I was getting up to open it again. I waited. Just as before no-one answered. Suppressing my irritation, I continued counting out the nightly floats.

There it was again. At least it had dwindled to a quiet tap.

Exasperated, I pushed back my chair. This was beyond a joke. I wrenched open the door, my anger much in evidence.

"What...!"

Anxious faces pulled instinctively back. I confronted two of my usherettes, Iris and Brenda.

"We've come for our programmes, Mrs Peacock," they said, hesitantly.

Behind them I could see the rest of the girls coming on duty.

I frowned. "Have you been up before?"

"No," Brenda said. "We've only just arrived."

"You didn't sound too pleased when we first knocked," Iris pulled a face, "so we waited a minute."

Looking at them I had to smile. "Let's just say your knock was the final straw. I've been up and down like a yo-yo all day long. Everytime I answered the door there was no-one about." I stood aside. "You'd better come in."

I even asked the Box Office to keep watch for me.

Handing a cash box over, I noticed them exchanging what I can only describe as a very 'knowing look'.

"What's the matter?" I watched them closely. "You've just met Charlie," said Brenda.

"Charlie?'

I'd only recently started work at the theatre and everyone had been most helpful and friendly, but I was sure no-one had mentioned Charlie.

"He goes around doing damn stupid tricks like knocking on doors then running away?" I enquired, my annoyance at the day's events rising again.

"Well, I wouldn't say he runs away..." said Brenda slowly.

To my surprise I found her now carefully watching me.

"But he must do," I said. "There's no-one there when I open the door!"

"No," Iris looked across at Brenda.

"Charlie is a ghost," Brenda said.

I stared from one to the other. "A ghost?"

They nodded.

A feeling I could well do without crept over me. It brought back childhood memories, eerie sounds in the house at night when the lights were out. I hadn't liked it then, and I wasn't thrilled now.

Ghosts! I could do without.

I stood looking at them, I felt I should be saying, 'don't be silly,' or, 'you're joking?' but remembering my day I had a gut feeling they were right.

Good grief! One week in my new job and already The Theatre Ghost was knocking on my door.

A ghost who had, to all intents and purposes, been christened by the staff and been given the name of 'Charlie'.

I heard many stories as time went by of staff either actually seeing Charlie himself, as a grey mist, or having an uneasy feeling of his presence.

Mrs Eve Rainforth is in her eighties now. She remembers seeing Charlie in 1943.

Eve was in charge of the front of house. In those days the public used to queue outside the building until it was time for the doors to open.

One night she was in the foyer with the manager waiting to open the doors. Observing the people in the queue she recalls thinking how strange one particular gentleman looked. He was tall and thin with a large prominent nose. He wore a dark grey riding coat, his long dark hair curling up at the ends and reached onto the cape of his coat. Wrapped around his neck was a coloured muffler.

When the foyer doors were open, Eve went outside to see him, but he had disappeared. Returning inside she told the manager about him. He hadn't seen the man and informed her that she had too vivid an imagination.

In those days the box office was along the back of the foyer, Mrs Rainforth's office was nearby at the side. As she returned to her office one day she began to have a 'queer feeling'. Walking past the people queuing for matinee tickets she saw the long grey riding cloak again. The same strange man she had seen before. He was waiting for an 'unreserved seat'. As she watched he disappeared. At the time of writing, at 88 years old, Mrs Rainforth remembers him clearly because he was so totally different.

Iris has been with the theatre since 1967 and now shares her experiences with Charlie.

Before refurbishment the way to the dress circle was through the circle bar and up central stairs.

One night Iris and Brenda were sitting on the back row of the dress circle. The performance had started, everyone was engrossed in the play.

Footsteps sounded, coming up the stairs. They both stood up together, turning round to see who was arriving late. There was no – one there.

Afterwards they wondered how they could have heard the footsteps when there was thick carpet down!

Coffee and the usual assortments of drinks were sold in the circle bar at the interval with two usherettes usually preparing the same when they had finished their duty on the doors.

Dorothy had the job at 7.30 of putting the cups and saucers out in rows ready for the interval rush.

Florrie, coming along a little later to boil water in two giant kettles on an antiquated stove. One night Iris, who was on duty on the dress circle door, heard crockery being put out on the counter earlier than usual at 7.15, and wondered why Dorothy had left her door duty so early. Iris went down to investigate. Frightened, she stopped in her tracks. It felt extremely cold and seemed misty. No-one was there and no cups or saucers were laid out. She felt a cold sweat over her. Turning she went back upstairs.

Later, she asked Dorothy if she had come up early, but she hadn't!

The next day at the matinee performance it was Iris' duty to open the circle bar doors, and put the lights on. This entailed walking across the dark room, going behind the counter to switch on the lights.

Remembering her experience of the previous evening she told Mrs Bristoe, who was the manageress, that unless someone came with her she daren't go.

Charlie's presence had been felt again.

Some time later in that same bar, Iris was sitting on a settee with two colleagues. Suddenly, across the room Iris saw a little grey-haired old man in a grey suit. Iris managed to point and shout out, but as she did so he disappeared! The other ladies hadn't seen him.

Maybe the theatre had two ghosts at that time, because that certainly wasn't Charlie. I wonder who the visiting ghost was?

At the very top of the theatre on either side of the upper circle are two large walk-in cupboards. Years ago they were used to store empty boxes. On one occasion Joan Body was on duty by herself in the upper circle. Iris was below her on the dress circle, and they were talking to each other just before the theatre opened.

Joan felt an icy draught. Suddenly, the doors nearest swung open. No-one came out. Rooted to the spot she watched, terrified, as the cupboard door squeaked open (it opens outwards) then gently closed by itself again. She felt the hairs on the back of her neck and head stand on end, her shoes, she recalls, felt as though they were nailed to the floor.

Iris, not knowing what had happened but seeing her face turn white and her hair stand on end, shouted up to see if she was alright.

Charlie had gone walkabout again.

Down in the basement at the other side of the theatre, Peggy Moran was the wardrobe mistress and busily working in the washroom next to the dressing rooms. This was the area that the cleaners always said was freezing cold. They used to say it was warm until they got to a certain point then it changed and always felt uneasy there. All the other dressing rooms were warm.

Peggy says this day she heard a 'swishing' noise, looked up and outside the door was a grey 'mass' moving along the corridor past her room.

She was transfixed, unable to move. When she thought it had gone she ran out to find the cleaners who were the only other people in the building.

"Whatever's the matter?" they asked. "You're as white as a sheet!"

When she managed to tell them what she had seen they didn't believe her! A week later someone saw the same thing come onto the stage!

Peggy was also wardrobe mistress when 'Snow White and The Seven Dwarfs' was the Christmas panto in 1982. She also looked after Dana, who played Snow White. Dana had a dressing room which was up a flight of stairs close to the stage and stage door.

Peggy and Dana continually heard knocks on the door but no-one was ever there.

One day they went upstairs, footsteps followed them, carrying on past them. Once again there was no-one there. The footsteps descended past the room again but still no-one was to be seen.

Brenda and I were standing at the back of the stalls watching a scene from the pantomime when the auditorium doors opened and closed. We both looked round but no-one came in. Then the ladies toilet door, which was at the back of the stalls before the refurbishment, also opened and closed.

That was it for me. I had to go into the auditorium on a night and turn the lights on, so Iris and Brenda came as well, believeing there was safety in numbers.

Jacqui Gower, one of the cleaners, saw Charlie early one morning when she was working in the lounge bar.

Sensing something there, she turned round. He was tall with wispy black and grey hair which reached past the collar on his grey travelling cloak. The ends of his hair were turned up.

He was standing behind the second set of pumps as though pulling himself a pint. He was sideways to Jacqui, his face with its prominent nose seemed the same colour as his cloak.

Jacqui was the one member of staff who didn't feel cold and wasn't frightened. She was just surprised and watched him for a while before he vanished.

About this time the cupboard in the upper circle had become the office storeroom and my changing room.

It seems relevant now that on many occasions I asked Geraldine Robinson to come up with me while I collected my things as I felt uneasy and didn't want to go on my own.

Geraldine and I used to be the last people out of the building, having to turn out the lights and lock up.

Sometimes it would be the other way around. I'd have Geraldine flying up to me saying there was this strange feeling in the lounge bar so she wanted to wait up with me until I was ready to leave.

We were a 'bright pair'. Both of us knew when the other had picked up this 'atmosphere' and was frightened, but we never put it into words until we were down the first corridor, then we'd both say 'RUN' and literally sprint out.

In those days the lighting was precarious. If someone had turned a switch off near the stage door it left the whole of the corridor winding down to the staff room in darkness. Once we'd turned our lights off and opened that door we were left with no way to see, plus two steps to go down.

Terrified, our hearts bumping, we would hold hands, carefully feeling our way. If we'd seen anything then I think the morning staff would have found us collapsed in a heap.

The horror we felt when we opened the door and found we had to go into a pitch black corridor, and then the utter relief when we saw a glimmer of light were two extremes neither of us will ever forget.

Darren Rothewell and three other people decided to see whether Charlie could be contacted with a ouija board. Nothing happened. No taps, just silence.

We hadn't a cellarman at the time, and Darren had struggled earlier in the day with a new beer delivery. He had stacked the barrels five high in a small store room we had.

Before the end of the evening the beer went off, so Darren came for a new barrel.

The storeroom door refused to open. Help was called, and between them they forced a space to squeeze through. To their amazement all the barrels stacked against the wall had been moved from the inside to block the entrance. I don't think they've used a ouija board since.

Councillors John and Ann Stanley are regular visitors to the theatre. They usually sit in seats EE 1 & 2. This is the back row of the dress circle on the left hand side facing the stage.

When they came to watch a military band they were unable to sit in their usual places and had seats on the other side of the theatre further forward in the dress circle.

During the performance Ann's attention was drawn to Box B not far away from her.

She watched as out of a grey mist a figure in a long cape emerged. It floated from inside the box, through the edge, continuing for about four feet suspended over the people in the stalls. The apparition then glided backward into the box then faded away.

Ann gasped and put a hand out to John.

"You've no need to tell me, I know what you're going to say," John said.

He hadn't seen anything, but he had felt icy cold. Ann said she hadn't felt cold just astonished at what she had seen.

Just before Christmas '92' Charlie seems to have started visiting again.

We have had knocks on our office door with no-one there. A glass falling off the ledge while the office was vacated. It had been in the same position all the morning. Instead of shattering it was in three large pieces.

Cardigans from off the chairs, books from the shelves. The kettle suddenly tipping over pouring water all over the floor while Iris was working at her desk.

My keys swinging continually in the door and various things being moved.

In Claire Elsdon's office which used to be Dressing Room C, they have a typewriter where the daisywheel suddenly starts wiggling round on its own.

Michael Lister, the deputy director, has been in the office when that has happened.

Anne Marie, Claire's assistant, came one morning believing another member of staff to be in the office using the computer as it was bleeping. When she finally opened the door the room was empty. The computer was signalling 'You have pressed an invalid key'.

Needless to say, she was greatly relieved when another member of staff arrived.

Sylvia Gallagher came to use the typewriter in this office while it was free.

She heard Claire's keys, which were behind her on the desk, being picked up and put down. She turned round to talk to Claire, but no-one was there.

Nowhere it seems is safe. A colleague who shall be nameless was in the disabled toilet in the stalls when the hand-drier opposite her started coming on and switching off non-stop. She swears that no-one in her position could have got out of there faster than she did.

The catering area seems another favourite haunt. June Brady was working at the kitchen table waiting for Julie Hall to arrive. She heard the footsteps, felt the touch on her shoulder in greeting (she thought).

"Hi, Julie!" June looked round, there was no-one there.

Sandra Hairsine, while working behind the lounge bar, has stood and watched glasses from further down the bar jump off the side and break. Yet from their positions on the shelf there was no way they could have just fallen.

Darren, alone in the lounge bar collecting glasses, noticed grey mist begin to form in the alcove under the clock. He didn't wait to see what it formed into, he hurtled up the spiral staircase to the foyer.

June Andrews seems to be a favourite with Charlie. Talking to Sandra one day, she said "There's somebody behind me!"

'No, there isn't! Carry on!"

With that, glasses behind June 'fell' off the shelf.

Regularly, June feels someone stroking her neck. She can even be talking to Sandra and tell her, "Someone's stroking me," and Sandra will say, "Therers no-one there!"

The classic was when June was sitting at the kitchen table and felt someone gently stroking her bottom. Turning round to see who was taking liberties, she looked straight at the wall her chair was pressed up against.

They say 'Gentlemen prefer blondes'. It seems in June's case even ghosts do as June is blonde.

The question to this day remains: Who is Charlie? However, in a quest to get a better look at who haunts the theatre, Lesley Howitt, accompanied by five lady members from The Friends of the New Theatre, decided that they would spend a night in the auditorium, their base being Box A.

So, armed with sleeping bags, pillows and flasks, they settled down for their vigil. Certainly the atmosphere was set, everywhere being pitch black, extremely cold, and very eerie. And if anyone needed to use the toilets then they went in pairs, no-one daring to move out of the box on their own.

Well, Charlie did not appear, but breakfast did, and a cooked one at that.

So, remember when next visiting the theatre, if you feel a sudden and eerie chill, then cast that glance behind, for you may meet Charlie, the theatre ghost.

PART THEE: COASTAL HAUNTINGS

"IT'S ONLY ME"

A short story now from Bridlington. The couple had been in the flats for about four or five months when the visitor called. Now Andy by description you would say, was without doubt a tough sort of chap and certainly not of a nervous disposition. But on the night of January 1st, 1990, he had a visitor that "shook him rigid".

Andy had been out to see a mate and arrived home as his wife was about to go to bed. He was hungry and cooked himself a few chips. It was whilst sitting in the kitchen enjoying his late night snack there suddenly appeared through the closed outside kitchen door the figure of a woman, saying as she came in "It's only me". Whoever she was, her words offered him no comfort as he fled upstairs leaving the rest of his chips behind.

Although not confirmed it is thought the apparition was that of a previous landlady who lived next door and used to come in saying "It's only me"!

THE BLONDE - GOOD LOOKING ROMAN SOLDIER

I don't doubt many of you will have heard that old saying about 'Fairies at the bottom of our garden', well I have never met anyone yet with fairies. However, I have heard through my friend Reverend Tom Willis about a lady who had a 'Blonde - good looking Roman Soldier' at the bottom of her garden! I wonder if any readers can beat that?!

Our spectator of this Roman ghost's appearances was a pleasant little Scottish lady living in Bridlington's Sewerby Road, who over a period of two or three years had four or five visitations from him. Her house was on flat land that gently sloped down and contained her garden.

It was during the months of June and October that he made his visits, usually at the time the lady was weeding in the bottom left-hand corner of her garden.

She had noticed a movement out of the corner of her right eye, and turned, to see what had distracted her. To her surprise it was a Roman Soldier, and no mistake at that. He was about 22 to 24 years old, blonde and good looking and wearing a brass or gold chest plate, a leather kilt, with what looked like brass bobbles on it. On his feet were sandals with criss cross thongs round his legs, but he wore no helmet and carried no sword.

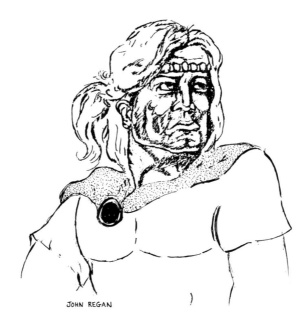

JOHN REGAN

On each visit to her garden the lady never once felt nervous or afraid of him. On the contrary, she thought he was 'quite dishy' and was fascinated by his appearances, feeling somewhat privileged at being able to see him and a bit of history unfold before her eyes. But she was certain he never knew she was there, and if he did he never showed it, although on one occasion he had looked rather startled, but still hadn't looked at his spectator.

Probably the strangest part about his visits was the fact he always seemed to be going somewhere from somewhere and walked up the slope of the garden disappearing into the edge of her house. However his walk didn't exactly correspond to the slope, he walked at a slightly different angle to that of the garden slope!

Investigations were later to reveal that where he had walked there had once been a Roman road running parallel to what is now the Sewerby Road, and thought to lead to a nearby Roman Camp somewhere along the cliff top, the remains of which sadly disappeared into the sea sometime during the 1890's.

On hearing this story, I commented about how I wished I could have seen what that soldier saw when he was in the garden. Did he see everything as it was in his time, or ours?

SCARBOROUGH'S HAUNTED SCHOOL

I have often thought that Scarborough must host a good collection of hauntings, but had heard of none until *The Hull Dally Mail* reported the strange happenings from a school in the old town quite close to that excellent landmark, the Castle.

Apparently, the school was built way back in 1896 on land that had once been occupied by a Franciscan Friary, this being confirmed by the discovery of the remains of monks (or to be more precise friars) in a graveyard whilst the school's foundations were being dug – those remains being removed to Hull for reinternment.

The Headmaster, who had been at the school for over eight years, never believed there were such things as ghosts, but in the December 18th 1989 edition of *The Hull Daily Mail* confessed "I have been forced to change my mind". So just what had brought about this change of mind? Although "rather indistinct" he had seen sufficient to recognise what appeared to him to be a Franciscan monk in a grey habit, but that's not all, for the wall clock in his study had often been moved, only to be found later under his desk! Chairs had also been moved as had an assortment of items in the school kitchen, and as often happens in haunted properties, the light had also been frequently switched on at times when there has no-one present in the building, causing concern from the local police.

Thankfully, these ghostly happenings have become almost accepted as part of the school's routine and cease to cause concern.

However, there is a foot-note to this haunting, for it appears the ghostly visitor isn't too keen on the school's Sunday activities. It was invariably after the school's use on Sundays that most of the reported occurrences happened!!

PART FOUR

SOUTH HUMBERSIDE

It was late in October 1992 when I was first approached by Steve Popplewell in his final year at the University of Humberside studying for a degree in Documentary Communication. So what was my use in this direction? Well, Steve was in the development stages for the production of a proposed video on the subject of ghosts and hauntings and how far society and the individual are involved and deal with ghosts. The project sounded fascinating and having an interest in the supernatural, Steve's discovery of my book had directed him towards me. I soon realised there would be demands on my time and knowledge and so we entered into an agreement: I would help in exchange for a pint and a ghost story or two. Well, at the time of writing I still have the thirst but that can wait for I have the haunting tales to tell and shall relate them to you through these pages as told by Steve.....

"The three stories were told to me by my girlfriend's Auntie Maureen who lives in Cleethorpes. Ghosts had somehow come up in the conversation whilst we were having Sunday dinner. Not your usual Sunday afternoon topic, I admit, but we all sat there for a good hour after the meal had ended listening attentively.

Apparently Maureen has always been very receptive to ghosts and such supernatural activity, believing quite genuinely that she is some kind of medium (although she never practices that 'art' as such). She tends to feel things and see things that others don't, a gift she says that has been handed down through the female side of the family for generations. Her mother was an active spiritualist and according to other sources such handing down of medium type powers is quite common.

As you read on, very early in the first story, you will realise that Maureen's sensitivity to her surroundings is very keen, for she feels something as soon as she enters the home of Mr and Mrs Fry.....But let me not spoil this story too much, for as I read it I felt a chill. On now to the nightly visits......."

THE NIGHTLY VISITS

Leaving home is a traumatic experience for any young person without any added complications. However when Maureen moved out of her parent's home at the age of nineteen she was to experience one of her more amazing ghostly episodes.

Maureen moved in with a local couple, Mr and Mrs Fry and their daughter, in a house on Grimsby Road in Cleethorpes. Despite the house being cosy and well cared for Maureen felt that there was something not quite right about the place. On entering the house she felt that something else occupied the home besides the family, but wanting to offend no-one she said nothing. Maureen was given the central bedroom at the top of the main staircase, it had a double bed, and another door at the opposite side of the room. This second door led to a second strangely dingy back landing where there was a bathroom, bedroom, and another staircase.

The first night Maureen stayed in the house Mrs Fry showed her to her room and said that if Maureen wanted to take a bath she was free to do so but she would wait upstairs until Maureen had finished. Mureen thought this was very strange thing to do but Mrs Fry explained that she just wanted to ensure that the door leading from Maureen's room to the back landing was shut and locked properly as she felt safer if it was!

When Maureen had finished in the bath Mrs Fry locked the bedroom's back door and told Maureen that if for any reason she felt scared then she must come and wake her up. Again Maureen felt this was a strange request but agreed and bade her new landlady goodnight.

A couple of hours passed, but the room felt cold and Maureen was unable to sleep. Laying on her side with her back to the door Maureen felt someone tucking in the bed sheets. Turning over and switching on the light to see who it was she was horrified to discover that no-one was there. Looking down she then noticed the shape of the hands as they made impressions in the eider down. Carefully they worked, the invisible hands tucking in the sheets down both sides of the bed. Terrified Maureen reached out to try and touch who or whatever it was that owned these ghostly hands. Still not seeing anything she was able to grab hold of a large hairy arm which could only have belonged to a large muscular man. So as not to disturb the handywork of the invisible visitor Maureen slid out of the top of the sheets and fled in great haste to her landlady's room. Shaking and scared Maureen asked whether Mr Fry had been in to tuck her in that night. However Mr Fry was still fast asleep in bed. After much persuasion Maureen finally agreed to try to get back to sleep,but not surprisingly she dozed very uneasily as this was not to be the end of the night's events! It was approximately one or two in the morning and Maureen still could not sleep. Slowly she became aware of footsteps coming up the back staircase towards her bedroom's back door. The family never used the back staircase and as a result it was never decorated or carpeted. Even the door downstairs that opened onto these stairs was blocked by a large sofa.

On the uncarpeted stairs the sound of a woman's high heeled shoes could clearly be heard. Steadily the footsteps approached, across the landing they came, towards Maureen's back bedroom door. Many would expect a closed door to hold no problems for the average ghost but this one stopped dead in its tracks. As Maureen lay in bed terrified the heavy brass door handle was turned two or three times. On discovering the door was locked, to Maureen's relief the footsteps were heard to turn and go back down the stairs and disappear.

Getting not a wink of sleep all night Maureen was quick to question her landlady at breakfast the next morning. However, Mrs Fry would say nothing until Maureen had told her exactly what she had experienced. On hearing the account Mrs Fry finally admitted that all her relatives had had the same experiences as Maureen while sleeping in that very room.

In its past the property had been a Co-Op rented house and rumour has it that a fisherman had killed himself in that very room. Unbelievably Maureen stayed in the house and slept in the same room every night. The ghostly hands never tucked her in again but every night someone could be heard to walk diagonally across the room wearing what sounded like clogs on their feet. (In the Past fishermen often wore clogs while working on the docks).

The high heels also came up the stairs every night but Maureen was always careful to make sure the door remained locked. Maureen also added that she would often lay awake until both her visitors had been and gone so as to make sure they did not wake and disturb her later.

Maureen's room was not the only room in the house that was frequented by ghostly goings-on. At any time during the day the heavy old front door would fly open. A strong gust of wind would then blow through the hallway, the living room door would open and the curtain that hung above the door would fly high into the air. This became so common that the family largely ignored it. Instead they would just say "Come in George, and close the door behind you." (George being the nickname the ghost had acquired over a period of time.) Being a polite ghost the door would indeed slam shut behind him!

Maureen stayed in the house until her marriage three years later. Mrs Fry, now in her early eighties left, with her husband, to move into a new flat in 1979. Maureen still sees the house quite often but according to Mrs Fry the present owners have seen and heard nothing of the ghostly visitors who once stopped by on a regular basis.

DADDY'S HOME

Summer was approaching with haste during May 1954 when Maureen's step-mother was away on holiday. On her departure she had asked Maureen to keep an eye on the house in Wendover Rise, Cleethorpes, which meant every evening Maureen would go round to the house and ensure all was as it should be.

It was approximatly seven thirty on this warm May evening and Maureen's new boyfriend had agreed to go with her to check the house. To their horror, as they arrived and opened the front door the hallway was filled with a thick mist that came halfway up the wall. The temperature too had also dropped dramatically. Maureen slowly entered the house with her boyfriend following closely behind. The mist had filled the entire downstairs of the house but it was in the dining room that Maureen discovered the reason. At first on entering the room she could see little as the curtains were all closed. Fumbling for the switch Maureen flicked on the light only to have revealed to her the image of a man leaning against the fireplace. Maureen recognised the man's clothes as those her Father had often worn prior to his death only a month before.

Aware now of his visitors the man turned to face the quivering couple standing in the doorway. Immediately Maureen recognised the man as the ghost of her deceased father. Whilst looking directly at Maureen the ghost lifted up its arms and with its palms upturned put them out towards her as if beckoning to her. The ghost said nothing but Maureen and her boyfriend were already fleeing the house at great, speed. Neither of them stopped running until they reached the end of the street. Once there, Maureen's boyfriend asked who the man was. Obviosly she replied that it was her Father. "I thought you said your Father had died only recently." he said genuinely puzzled, and obviosly quite afraid. "He did" replied Maureen!

It was now that Maureen reluctantly realised that she had not ' locked the front door on her hasty retreat from the house and that she would now have to return and do so. After her boyfriend had flatly refused to accompany her Maureen nervousely approached the house alone. Easing the door open again she saw the mist was no longer there but the house still felt icy cold. Going back to the dining room she found that it too was back to normal. Turning out the light she left and locked the door behind her.

Despite returning to the house every evening Maureen never saw the ghost again, nor did her step-mother when she returned from her holiday. Maureen was always considered to be her Father's favourite and she now believes her Father had only returned to see if his daughter was alright.

MOTHER'S LITTLE HELPER

Like many children, I could never bring myself to go upstairs without first turning on the landing light. After seeing her first ghost at the age of eight Maureen had more reason than most to feel apprehensive about doing the same!

It was early evening and Maureen was sent to get ready for bed. It was only when she got halfway up the stairs that she realised someone was at the top of them. Looking upwards to the top of the stairs she saw a woman in a green side-rouch dress, holding hands with two young children. Holding her right hand was a young blonde haired girl with a basket of beautiful flowers on her arm. Clutching to the woman's left hand was a young boy, slightly taller than the girl.

Without saying a word the woman let go of the children's hands and with her palms facing upwards, she put her arms out towards Maureen beckoning her to come to her. At seeing this Maureen screamed and lept from the stairs, the noise prompting her Father to come rushing in. She described what she had seen but the apparitions had vanished. However Maureen's Father recognised the description of the green dress and took Maureen upstairs. There tucked among the old clothes in her Mother's wardrobe, was the green dress worn by the ghost.

Maureen's Mother had died two years previously at the age of thirty three, and had been bed-ridden ever since Maureen's birth. Satisfying herself, with some relief that the ghost that she had seen was that of her deceased Mother, Maureen could still not explain the two children at her mother's side.

Since that time Maureen has seen many spiritualist mediums who, without any knowledge of the ghosts on the stairs, have told her that they see a young blonde-haired girl carrying a basket of beautiful flowers at Maureen's side! They have also said this girl will be with Maureen until the day she too passes away but no mention has ever been made of the young boy. Maureen's Mother only had two children, perhaps the young boy now walks by the side of her other child, Maureen's brother!

PART FIVE:

MISCELLANEOIUS EAST YORKSHIRE HAUNTINGS

THE STRANGER IN BLACK

The note from Doreen requested me to contact Dick Robinson the gardening correspondant for the *Beverley Guardian*. I knew Dick had been writing the Gardening column for a great many years, and wondered could he possibly have heard of my newly acquired 'green fingers', why not? I thought, I always keep my lawn looking good.

My return call to Dick soon dispelled any aspirations I had of my gardening expertise being required for his column, no this time my expertise as a researcher of ghostly tales was to benefit.

Dick Robinson's Grandmother. Florence Silversides, was born at

Kilnwick, a small village between Beverley and Driffield, and was the daughter of the village blacksmith, Robert Silversides. Grandma's ghostly experience was frequently told to Dick and throughout its many tellings never, ever varied in its content.

The year is believed to have been 1883, when one Sunday afternoon the then young Florence along with her Mother and Father set off from Kilnwick by pony and trap to Kirkburn to visit a friend who was very, very ill.

Florence sat at the side of her Father who was driving, whilst his wife Rachel Anne, sat behind with her back to the others.

It was whilst they were on the grass track that runs to Bracken Farm and Bainton that they noticed a man dressed in black astride a black horse, coming towards them. When the pony and trap drew level with the stranger, Florence's Father raised his hat and bid him 'Good Afternoon', to which there was no reply. At the same moment the pony shied and Mother in the back upon hearing the voices, turned to see who her husband had spoken to, but was surprised to see there was no-one there. The stranger had disappeared!

Upon their arrival at their friend's house, sad news awaited them, death had already visited the household taking their friend's life.

As a youngster, Dick Robinson and his friends never failed to be fascinated by Grandma's telling of this tale and he often asked her if that stranger had disappeared by riding off into a field or nearby wood and she always assured Dick that he had not, yet could offer no explanation for his sudden disappearance, but she always reminded him that both she and her Father (and the pony judging by its reaction!) had obviously seen him even though Mother saw nothing.

Thanking Dick Robinson for his story, as is usual, I said that should he hear any more stories. I would appreciate him passing them on. No sooner had I said this than he asked if I would like to hear one from South of the Humber, which had been related to him by a work colleague, Richard, who had lived on the South Bank at either Barton or Barrow.

One afternoon Richard along with his Mother and Father sat in their front room, Richard and his Mum were sitting facing the window. when quite unexpectedly Mother saw a relative at the window. "That's strange, she lives in Canada". Despite the surprise appearance at the window, Richard's Mum went to open the door and welcome their surprise visitor. Her initial surprise soon turned to concern when she saw no-one was there. This left Richard and his Mum somewhat disturbed as they both had had a good view of her.

However, the reason for this mysterious appearance and disappearance of the relative soon became apparent, for a few days later a telegram arrived informing them that their relative in Canada had died!

Dick Robinson then suggested we contact his son John who we were assured would only be too pleased to share his experience with us and so follows John's story.

Back in 1968, John was working at the Longhill Nurseries in Hull. The complex was fairly new, it being built around 1961-62 The layout of the building consisted of a long corridor with greenhouses branching off to the south side and the boiler rooms and stores on the north side. John recalls that it was sometime during October or November and is certain that it was late Friday afternoon when his experience occurred, for he was pushing his truck full of tools back to the greenhouse store in the centre of the complex, ready to pack up for the day. As he approached the store he became aware of a movement, but thought it was one of the women from the adjoining florist's department. As he entered the storeroom he was greeted by a sight he has not forgotten to this day; in front of him was the shape of a figure,

R DESBOROUGH

not distinguishable as a man or woman, it had the appearance of a black net curtain. John stood rooted to the spot, at the same time feeling a cold wind pass his face as the apparition moved very quickly past him disappearing through the wall at the far end of the store. Badly shaken by this experience, he eventually managed to return to where his work colleagues were and told them what he had seen and became even more unnerved as he was to learn that one of them had been working one night when he had heard footsteps, only to discover that no one was there.....

Though John has not seen or heard of anything else at Longhill Nurseries since, he remembers that day very clearly and also pointed out that the building was very well illuminated at that time so there was definitely no mistaking what he saw!!

THE BEDROOM VISITOR

This haunting is from a residential home for the elderly situated in East Yorkshire, its location not being revealed at the request of the staff.

The home is a large three storey house with staff accommodation in the attic level of the building. The staff have the benefit of their own common room and bedroom, which is of course ideal for duty staff on shifts and as an 'on call' room.

Over a period of time, several of the staff had complained of there being an eerie and uneasy feeling in the staff common room, but found it more in evidence in their bedroom. The unease felt in these rooms came to a head one night as one of the staff slept.

As you know, being awakened suddenly is no joke, but just imagine being awakened to find a man, a complete stranger, pulling the bedding off your bed! The woman pulled them back, he pulled again! She was certain it was an intruder and to escape from the room she would have to push past him! In panic she 'flung' herself out of bed, to rush towards the door, but as she did she thrust out her arm to push the intruder to one side ...... her arm passed straight through him! That added greatly to her speed of departure, screaming as she headed downstairs. That intruder wasn't real - he was a ghost!

Well, it appears the night's event hadn't disturbed the home's residents, but besides one very upset and unnerved victim, the rest of the staff were uncomfortable about spending time alone in their quarters.

Help was sought. The Reverend Tom Willis was called, their story being told to him about their bedroom visitor, and the uncomfortable coldness that prevailed in their rooms.

A blessing was necessary to cleanse the rooms of any disturbed spirits.

Tom proceeded with the blessing and whilst in one room, three of the staff were leaning against a wall listening to him. It was when Tom reached the part in the blessing where he 'commanded anything disturbed to go and the peace of God to return to the room' that Tom noticed the three staff suddenly move away from the wall. Later Tom asked them why they moved as they did, the reply was that the wall had begun to get warmer, and each had felt a pleasant warmth return to the room in place of the usual unpleasant chill that had been around for so long. And from that day the home and staff went about their business in apparent peace.

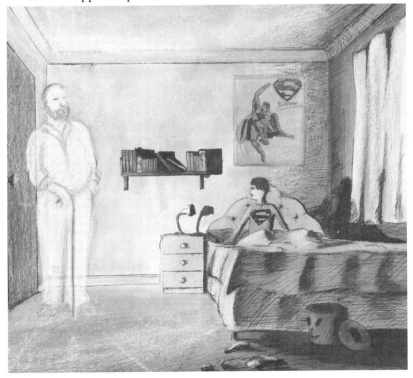

THE GARDENER - MY FATHER ?

I have always appreciated the trust people have had in me when sharing their haunting or ghostly experiences, and in some cases they have been of a very personal nature and yet I have always been somewhat reserved when it came to telling mine, strange isn't it? So, from my personal collection comes this story.

Mother one day casually mentioned that on numerous occasions a very pleasant fragrance had drifted past her, as she sat in our living room. Thinking, then saying I thought it probably originated from either after–shave or cologne I may have been using upstairs, the fragrance permeating the rooms below; but Mother was adamant saying that this particular smell was not mine! and although she couldn't describe it accurately, said it was more a smell of a beautifully fragrant garden. I recall suggesting that it may be our garden, but Mum also dismissed that idea.

I hadn't smelt it. so couldn't offer any additional explanations, that is until the day I was sitting on the chair arm searching through one of the side-board drawers. Suddenly, I shivered, I wasn't cold. then I discovered 'that' smell. It teased my nostrils, and was an unusually pleasing floral fragrance of the like I had not smelt before. l knew then it wasn't from our garden.

Sometime later, I related our 'smelly' story to a friend who was aware of my interest in the supernatural. Without hesitation she asked if I knew of anyone "to do with gardens" who had either lived or died in the house as she thought they could be visiting us. I do not know if it was because a possible explanation was so close to me, but for some inexplicable reason my mind hadn't directly associated the fragrance with my late Father. who before he entered industry had been a professional gardener and right up to his death had maintained an enthusiastic interest in gardening!

THE JOKER

Tom Willis had been talking to the Priory Church Youth Club and asked at the end if there were any questions. One girl then went on to tell Tom of an experience her mother and brother had with a very vivid ghost in their house. The girl went on to say that her brother was a very lively character and how when he was about six or seven years old he would come down to breakfast and crack some joke or conundrum with the family. When asked where he got them from, he would reply by saying "from the old lady".

The family would humour the lad saying "What, the old lady who comes into your room every night?" and he would reply by saying "Yes, she tells me all sorts of stuff".

The family didn't take much notice of this, even though on occasions he could be heard laughing loudly and chattering away in his room. Still they never bothered him, he was such a 'live wire' and certainly no-one thought there was anything wrong with him. It was even thought he had invented a friend to talk to, something they knew youngsters often did.

Until the night his mother had listened outside his bedroom door to him chattering away to 'his old lady'. She wasn't unduly perturbed at first. Then she heard what she thought was a voice replying! Slowly and quietly she opened the door and went in. To her astonishment, there sat on the bed was her son thoroughly engrossed listening to an old lady sitting on his bed. She wore a nightgown and a wide brimmed hat! Both were talking away to each other and took no notice of mother who by now felt as though she was an intruder, and crept out again.

When mum challenged her son about the old lady, his reply had been to say "Now do you believe me?".

In an attempt to find out who the old lady was, they researched the history of the house, to discover that she had had the house before them and had been trying on the large-brimmed hat whilst in her nightgown, had sat down in an armchair and died.

THE FACELESS ONE

For quite a few weeks the *Beverley Guardian* had been reproducing stories from our second Ghost Book. The story they used on December 1st was from the 'Hessle Hauntings' including the strange happenings around the Jenny Brough Lane area. The following week the *Beverley Guardian* carried a letter from a Mrs Helen Trott of Boothferry Road Hessle. Her reply read as follows: "A couple of years ago my daughter was riding her pony (normally a very sensible animal) along the bridle path which passes Tranby Coft. Just before they reached the water tower, Smoky suddenly started snorting and acting up.

My daughter, Claire, urged her forward, but she refused to move.

Suddenly, from the right of the path a small boy appeared. crossing in front of my daughter and her pony. In his hand he appeared to be carrying a parchment. Claire said he turned to look at her. but there was no face. On further questioning, he appeared to be in old-fashioned dress, but did not appear to have any legs visible.

On this happening the pony reared, turned and galloped all the way home, my daughter unwilling and unable to stop her. I have not any doubt in my mind that something very strange happened up there – I saw the terrified state of the pony and my daughter would not go anywhere alone for days, terrified that the apparition would follow her home.

I have talked to many elderly people in this area who all say they know of the ghost of a child in this area, but no-one knows the story behind it. I now wonder if my daughter was mistaken and the 'boy' was in fact a girl."

I 'phoned Mrs Trott firstly to acknowledge her letter which adds more support to the Hessle hauntings and at the same time asked her if there was any more detail she could add to her story – sadly there was not.

.......and more

Two years after hearing that last story my nephew Paul Robinson told me the following, and adding to the collection even more strange happenings from the Jenny Brough Lane area.

Rachel was about 10 years old when she first experienced a haunting. It was one afternoon in late Autumn when she arrived home from school and whilst closing the dining room curtains she saw the figure of a tallish person she thought to be a woman. The stranger was standing in the garden about 10 feet away from Rachel who could see clearly that the person was wearing a long hooded brown cloak but appeared to have no face. Upset and frightened by this 'person' lurking in the garden, the young Rachel fled to her room in tears and dared not even tell her parents what she had seen, fearing they wouldn't believe her!

About two years later Rachel recorded her second brush with the supernatural. She had awakened early one morning feeling exceptionally cold, and opening her eyes to the morning light that filtered into her room through the curtains, saw standing there that same figure she had seen in the garden a couple of years earlier. Rachel stared, her eyes painfully transfixed on the apparition for what seemed like an age, before it eventually disappeared.

Three years passed before Rachel had her third haunting experience. This time it was a fine Spring evening with a gentle mist to soften the fresh greens of fields and hedges. Rachel rode her horse on its daily exercise along the bridle path that cuts between the Tranby Croft and Jenny Brough Lane, in that tranquil stillness of the evening Rachel watched the path passing below her, then looklng up was suprised to suddenly see a woman walking towards her. Nothing odd about that you may think, except that she wore a long hooded gown that trailed along the ground and she looked somehow familiar. Rachel watched her draw closer, that was until the horse had to negotiate a narrow opening causing Rachel to look away momentarlly, and in that brief time the woman had disappeared completely. But the horse became distressed and started to fret, at the same time breaking into a profuse sweat and began walking backwards, a good four minutes passing before the horse's confidence could be restored again .

Into late 1990, Rachel was once again on that same pathway where she had seen the woman, and again the horse reacted in a distressed manner as it had done previously. On this occasion even though no-one was seen the horse's mood brought back that previous memory to unnerve Rachel.

We have to go back now to 1989 and into Rachel's house again. Her parents were out, only she and her younger brother remained in the house, Rachel upstairs in her room while her brother played his violin in the dining room downstairs.

From upstairs Rachel could hear the strings being teased, then silence! followed by a scream, then the sound of her brother crying loudly. Rushing downstairs Rachel found her brother very distressed and unable to tell what had upset him. Well, eventually Rachel did discover his problem. He told that whilst he played his violin someone had appeared from nowhere and had been standing behind him...... Was it the cloaked woman again? The poor boy's fear was such that his description didn't make sense, but suffice to say it had given him a scare.

THE NIGHT CALLER

During the late eighties, Reverend Tom had been requested to visit a house in Willerby where the occupants were experiencing some strange 'goings on'. The family comprised of mother, father, their two children, a boy and a girl. Their problem was that various items in the home were disappearing, or as they thought they kept losing them. Once or twice it's easy to misplace things, but this was happening all too frequently. The boy and girl were worst affected, their property would disappear then later re-appear in places already searched!

The girl's pyjama case was just one item from a catalogue of things that vanished from her room. Mother suggested that she must have misplaced it, daughter said not, and searched everywhere without success. Then a few days later mother was in the girl's bedroom and saw that the pyjama case was back on her pillow, and told her daughter who said it hadn't been there previously adding that someone or something must have put it back, as it had definitely been lost. The children blamed each other, suspecting each of playing practical jokes, both denied such a thing.

Then one night something even stranger happened. They had a visitor unknown and unexpected. The husband had gone to work his night shift, the children had gone to bed and his wife retired also. Now from the days of the children been younger, mum had always left the bedroom door open just in case they should ever want their parents, or cry out during the night. All these years later she hadn't dropped the habit. The bedroom door remained open and she slept with her back to the open door.

Not sure of how long she had been in bed, mum was suddenly disturbed by the light being switched on. Thinking it was one of the children wanting something she turned over and was astonished to say the least to see an old man looking round the door at her. His face too expressed a look of amazement and appeared embarrassed at seeing her. He left, switching the light off as he went. Although her reaction was a bit slow, mum shot out of bed, put the light back on and proceeded to check the house over. She found no-one and there was no sign of anyone having gained access to the property. All the doors and windows were still secure.

Later, when her husband returned home, a second search of the house was made. Everywhere was still secure.

Tom blessed the house and to this day has thankfully heard nothing further from them.

THE SPORTS CAR

It was night, the young man and his girlfriend were chatting away as they drove along the winding bit of the Bridlington to Filey road, to be more accurate the section between the roundabout near Muston and Filey.

The driver noticed headlights in his mirror and the car they belonged to was moving fast. Realising this hasty driver may want to overtake he kept close to the left allowing him plenty of room to pass.

The overtaking car was remembered as being green or certainly a dark colour and an old-fashioned sports job. The car drew level and slightly overtook, then disappeared!

The young man turned to his girlfriend and asked if she had just seen what happened, she had. He stopped the car, both getting out, expecting to find an accident. They looked over the hedge but there was no sign of headlights, no crashed car, nothing at all!

THE HAUNTINGS OF CHARLIE

Before the last war when Charlie was 16, he worked on a farm at Carnaby and one night he was going back from Bainton to the farm along Boynton Hall's carriage track.

"It was dark but I remember my carbide lamp on the bicycle was flaring as I cycled down the centre of the track, desperately trying to keep out of the wheel ruts as I went along."

'Going hell for leather' down the track I was going through the wood with rows of trees on either side. Suddenly a man stepped out from behind a tree! There was no way I could have stopped, certainly not at the speed I was travelling, and I didn't, not even when I hit him. But there was no impact, I just passed straight through him!! I was terrified and didn't dare look back, but kept on going as fast as I could.

All winter I avoided that route, only daring to return again during the summer and the return of light nights.

The war over and I believe it was 1952 or 53. I remember I was living at Muston, and lt was one moonlight night around 10 o'clock as I walked back home after I had visited the cinema in Filey.

I had come onto the maln Scarborough to Bridlington road and was walking up towards the turn off for Muston, when from the Scarborough direction I heard the sound of an old motorcycle coming towards me. Sure enough it drew closer and rounded the corner, and although displaying no lights I clearly saw there were two men sitting on the machine. Both wore goggles and leather helmets. As they passed I stared, quite fascinated by this sight, until suddenly they disappeared!

Convinced no-one would believe what I had seen I kept these experiences to myself." Thanks Charlie for sharing both your hauntings with us.

THE SPIRIT OF WOODHOUSE FARM CONTINUES....

Throughout my years of research into stories of ghosts and hauntings there have not been many I have not liked, although one in particular I heard left me feeling so uncomfortable that I was unable to further my researches. There was just something about the story that had a more than usual sinister 'feel' to it, and yet it would have been an incredible story to tell. Sorry dear reader, on this occasion I must deny you that chill. However, the following story is a continuation of one told in "More Ghosts and Hauntings" and although nowhere as sinister as the one I have kept from you I find this one leaves me feeling uncomfortable whenever I think about it, and as you read on I'm sure you too cannot fail to feel a fraction unnerved when you know that this particular haunting moves with the bricks from a once haunted house.

The original story was told to me by a friend David Bowman and was faithfully re-told in his own words in the second collection of hauntings.

Briefly, and our telling goes back to the 1950's, the owner's son always slept in his parents' room. This was thought to be somewhat strange as his was the only bedroom with a wooden floor and as such was the warmest room! but the door was always kept locked!

The Bowman family moved in, and Mr Bowman's brother, who was to work on the farm prior to his National Service duty, was given that unused boy's room!

However, each morning that he awoke Mr.Bowman found the trapdoor in the ceiling was open – strange, because it had to be pushed up and lifted over a ridge. Upon being questioned as to why he repeatedly lifted it he adamantly denied touching it. Realisation then began to dawn as to why the boy of the previous family had always slept in his parents' room! No doubt was in anyone's mind that their house had a ghost!

It was then decided that Mr Bowman should use another room, his 'old' room being locked again. However, each morning the room was opened to reveal the open trapdoor.

The stairs creaked on certain steps so when footsteps were heard on the stairs the family member would watch, hoping to catch a glimpse of their ghost, but never did. However, they were sure their alsatian did, for its eyes would move as though following something or someone moving across the room.

The door between the passage and the kitchen had a large gap under it and often the shadows of feet could be seen moving in the passage. This was especially noticable when the sun shone brightly, the unnerving thing was they knew the shadows were those of no-one they knew!

Both David and Paul were born in the farmhouse and strange as it may seem the ghostly activity almost ended and that trapdoor rarely moved. In fact a great peace existed in the house, that was when the Bowmans put thought into believing their ghost may have been that of a woman who had died in childbirth or possibly lost children of her own!

In the Spring of 1957 the Bowmans left the farm and initially feared a re-awakening of the hauntings, but as the new family had children they departed with confidence that things would be alright.

The youngest son, Paul, was always drawn to the farm and when home from London would drive out to look at it. The last time he saw the Farmhouse the windows had been boarded up. Curious as to the building's future Paul enquired from two occupants of a caravan in the farmyard to learn that the house was now unsafe and was to be demolished in the near future. Explaining that the house had been his birthplace, he was allowed access for a last look round, his curiosity beckoning him to what had been the 'little boy's bedroom'. The door had been locked, but the key was still there. On entering his eyes were instantly drawn to that trapdoor, wooden battens had been nailed across to securely hold it in place. It was obvious that things had happened again after they had left the farm.

Paul's discovery of the secured trapdoor brought a sadness from the Bowman family, a sadness in denying the spirit the freedom of movement as they had done.

The farmhouse was eventually demolished during the late seventies with David, the eldest son, collecting a number of bricks to keep as a reminder of the farm.

David kept three of those farmhouse bricks, a decision he has had reason to regret over the many years since the occupancy of his newly built bungalow in Pocklington.

This may take some believing but something came with, or in those bricks, for the Bowmans were to find at night their trapdoor to the loft space would be in place when they went to bed, but repeatedly they found that the morning following the trapdoor would have been pushed up and slid over into the loft. And that wasn't all, for David's wife, relatives and friends all experienced shadows and footsteps that had once been part of that old farmhouse!

But wait, there is still more, for when the Bowmans went on holiday the house keys were left with David's Mother-in-law, Doris, so she could keep watchful eye on the house. However, on one visit a surprise awaited Doris, for she found all moveable objects had been upended, the bird cage was laid on its side across the floor, plants had been strewn all over, also the ornaments were on their sides. It was as if a strong gust of wind had blown through and tipped everthing over. Naturaly Doris checked all doors and windows, first suspecting a burglary, but everything was found secure!

1979 saw the birth of the Bowman's daughter, and as had happended at the farm everything calmed down again, that is until they moved and took those bricks.

This time, though, David was wise after the event and left those haunted bricks in the garage which was attached to the house, and believing it to be the best place for them!

Maybe it was, but then was it, for almost immediately they started to hear loud bangings on the living room, wall, sufficient to cause

David to rush into the garage to investigate – needless to say he never found the cause of the noise. The years passed and the banging ceased, and that was the end of the story...... or was it, remember that spirit seemed to need a home.

The Farmhouse had been demolished in the mid 1980's and eventually a new bungalow was constructed nearby. The downstairs front room of the old farmhouse had been preserved and converted into an outside store room.

The owners, as in early 1991, bought both farm and bungalow in June 1988 and over the years have built up a thriving pig unit.

It was during 1990 that David Bowman received a phone call from the then owners of the farm, the lady of the house enquiring as to whether the story David had reported in the Second Book of Ghosts and Hauntings was true. David of course confirmed his story to be correct and could add support through numerous people who would verify what he had told. The lady was shocked because certain happenings that had occurred within her bungalow mirrored what had happened at both the farmhouse and David's home.

Now the story continues, and in David's own words: "Strange happenings started soon after Mr & Mrs X, along with their daughter, moved into the bungalow. As Mr, X spent some time abroad the daughter slept in her mother's bedroom. In the morning the loft cover, which was in the daughter's room, would be found to be off and pushed right back into the loft space, this having happened on numerous occasions. Oddly though, nothing happens to the loft when the daughter sleeps in her own room!"

"Another inexplicable event occurred one night when loud banging was heard on the outside wall of the bungalow. Mr X, naturally concerned, got up to investigate but found nothing to be the cause. Somewhat puzzled he returned to bed switching off the lights on the way. It wasn't long before the banging started. Again he got up to investigate, but now all of the lights he had switched off earlier were on!

'Well, look and search as they could no explanation for the banging has been found and it's not only the bungalow residents who experience it, for numerous friends who have stayed overnight have also been awakened by the mysterious sounds. `

"The loud banging on exterior walls reflects exactly what happened in both the home of my parents and of course my own home".

"It's a mystery without satisfactory answers, but there are some things all the properties have in common. All have been built over the past 20 years but probably the most important link between the bungalow at Woodhouse Farm, my parents' home and mine is, and have you guessed yet, we all have bricks in our homes from the original Woodhouse Farm! The bungalow has them built into its fire-place surround!"

"Thankfully, as I write this in 1991 all has been quiet at Woodhouse Farm now for almost a year and even longer with us."

Thank you David for re-telling your story, but David has omitted to mention his brother who also held some bricks from the Old Farm. However, I understand he left these and his problems behind him when he moved house, and has declined to comment upon his bricks, so now some new house owner has probably discovered they too share the spirit of Woodhouse Farm!

Well that's it, probably not the creepiest haunting you will read, but I'm sure you will agree it's not the most comfortable to go to bed with either.

CASTLE HILL CROSSROADS

I'm going back to about 1982 with this story, and must admit I had let this happening slip to the back of my mind, but have never forgotten it.

For many years I believed what we saw was real, and only fate saved lives from what could have been a very nasty accident, and although we both suffered shock for many months, the event of that day couldn't have really happened.

It was a Saturday morning around 10.30. I had collected my eldest nephew from his home in Kirkella and drove towards Beverley. As I entered the actual Castle Hill on the A164 just past the right turn to the hospital (before the roundabout), I braked slightly as I entered the hill, and have since so often thought of the consequences if I hadn't, but then I also ask myself the question would it, or did it make any difference? For on that day I'm sure we drove through a motor cyclist and pillion passenger Or did they pass through us?

You see, as we reached the bottom of that hill at the crossroads a motorcyclist and pillion passenger crossed in front of my car bonnet travelling right to left. Now as I write this these year's on I can still 'see' in my mind and shiver at that memory of that crossing of my path. We both saw it, and what made it so frightening was the closeness. We couldn't possibly have missed them, nor could they have missed us. Thankfully there was no accident, and strangely there was no sound, and neither of us saw where the phantom motorcycle and passenger went! My nephew and I often talked about our near miss, but only remembered our vision in dark grey/black. Has any reader ever heard of a ghostly motorcyclist and passenger who crosses that crossroad? I'd be pleased to hear from anyone who had, as an experience of the likes isn't easily forgotten.

A WARNING
THE EXORCISM

Mention the word exorcism and I'll wager practically everyone conjures up the Hollywood image, you know the scene, as the man of God comes to cast out the evil spirits, all hell breaks loose, and the special effects department have their field day, gales blow, walls and windows shake and all manner of strange things happen to people, not to mention the display of disturbed and upset apparitions as they depart this earth. Certainly as presented through the entertainment world it can be a sinister but spectacular display.

I had for a number of years been curious about what happened at an exorcism. Was it as the film makers portrayed or what? So when Tom told me of a newly reported haunting in Beverley and a request by the property users for Tom to exorcise it, I immediately asked if I could also go along.

To be honest, I didn't expect anything on the scale Hollywood could produce, not even for a 'B' feature film, but I did hope I could sense the presence by a chill or at the very least a tingle or two.

Unfortunately,we have been asked not to identify the property or even its whereabouts in the town, but the only clues I can give are that the present buildings were erected on the site of a once large and important manufacturing industry in Beverley.

Going back to Tom's initial report, he had been told that apparitions had been seen by both the present and previous occupants of the building, but it was the present users who were far from happy about what they had inherited.

One description was that of a man peering through one of the internal windows, his face in a sort of shimmer, another was thought to be that of a man rushing through the building, whilst on another occasion a man appeared spread-eagled floating high up on the wall, his face partially shrouded in a strange shimmer. In fact that apparition was described as being more like an eagle with a man's face, and as well as the occupants feeling generally uneasy about being in the place, they have also found their toilet door frequently locked from inside with no occupant!

Tom arranged a date and time for the blessing; introductions over, and a brief history of the site followed. This was to reveal that four people had tragically died in the site's industrial past, resultant in crushing to death and electrocution!

Tom then proceeded to carry out his blessing of the building to send out any unwelcome visitors. Having seen our house blessed I had a rough idea of what to expect, but then our house wasn't haunted.

On every wall and door Tom made the sign of the cross and didn't forget the stairs either, at the same time sprinkling Holy Water on the floor as he went. Regrettably, the names of the deceased were not known, for had they been, then Tom would have mentioned them in his prayers, but not knowing who or what these disturbances were Tom prayed for a veritable assortment of potential causes as follows, "all departed souls, all restless spirits, all evil presences, all souls in torment with bitter memories, phantasms, evil influences, magic powers and mind forces". Quite a list as you can see. He prayed for them to depart, and for "the restoration of the peace of God upon the place always".

Remember what I said earlier about the film makers' impressions of exorcisms? Well, as we followed Tom around the building, one of the company's three associates whispered to me, "don't they sometimes sort of appear and whoosh out?" On this occasion they didn't, none of us felt or saw anything, and I must admit to being a bit disappointed at not even feeling a chill or tingle.

Regardless though, the experiences seen and felt by the male users of that building had been sufficient to unnerve them to the point of seeking help.

Sincere thanks were extended to Tom for his help, who acknowledged with a warning, for as we discovered during the proceedings, two out of the three men had in years past tampered with the occult!

Tom's warning was a serious one, advising them at their peril not to dabble again and to the chap who also admitted to being a 'bit psychic', he was told not to interfere with the forces he could not understand or control.

I felt with their recent experiences they had been sufficiently warned. We left them and their premises, we hope, in peace.

****

So now I end this the third collection of ghosts and hauntings and fittingly on an exorcism. There are forces around us that few understand and when the inexperienced tap those forces for fun they can end up as the recipients of very unpleasant and long lasting consequences, and 'it' may be enjoyable reading about others affected, but it's no fun if it's you. I hope you enjoyed our journey through these 'haunted' pages, but please discourage and resist temptation to interfere with things you do not understand.